the Creator of this earth namely Kittung, on the other, there is co-existent a belief in many gods leading the author to a similar conclusion characterising these Soaras as having a religion of spiritism. Actually the pantheon of the Soaras is only a clever way of talk, so Elwin believes, because in practice these gods have a status of devils or supernatural forces only! To him, (Elwin) most of these deities are 'drinkers of blood'! As it is the case in the other study, I think the inability to understand the tribal religions here also is because of the author's bias in favour of one or another so-called 'organised' religion. Note the following observation about the Soaras.

"There is no idea of a supreme and beneficient Creator of all things. Where the Soaras have been free from Hindu influence, nothing is known of a beneficient deity". Then again, "only few of the gods receive anything like regular worship. Fewer have shrines created in their honour. Some are not worshipped at all. Many of them are remembered only at times of crises". Verrier Elwin sees Kittung, the Creator of the Universe, according to the Soaras, as "lacking in many of the attributes which the more highly developed religions have given to the Supreme Being. He is not omnipotent, omniscient or omnipresent". Therefore the author concludes, "the Soaras cannot create a perfect God". Accordingly, "Soara religion is rather weak."

Roy Burman's account of the religion of the Koragas of Karnataka is mainly an account of the ghosts, devils and 'bhutas'. Although he concedes, they report themselves as Hindus, (Census, 1961), "but the brand of Hindu religion followed by them at present has certain overtones of religious practices which have been termed as 'devil worship' ". Note the following :

"The 'bhuta' or spirit can be divided into two categories. (1) The 'bhutas' common for the community as a whole, (2) spirits of the dead ancestors who are supposed to exercise great influence on the well-being of the members. The principle 'bhuta' is 'Kuladeva' or 'patron-deity'. They are worshipped in time of birth, marriages etc. There are other 'bhutas' which are represented by images of stone symbolising different animals. There are also female 'bhutas'. The family 'bhutas' are kept inside the house over a wooden bracket known as 'bhutasthan'. The important 'bhutas' in the community are collectively worshipped at least once a year. The worship is performed at a consecrated spot under a tree. They place before the image of the bhuta, cooked rice mixed with turmeric powder, five betel leaves and liquor. They burn incense and sacrifice fowls and pigs. They perform dances and some divination".

The persistence of the animistic framework for the study of tribal religions in our country is not really surprising. It is part of the general phenomenon of the persistent domination of imperialist modes of thinking in most other spheres.

As in other parts of India the launching of anthropological studies in the context of north-east India was the product of British expansion over India during the 19th century. The need to govern the tribes of various races and vastly different cultures created in the rulers the need to study the life and culture of the ruled. "As European knowledge of the non-European world increased and as societies were formed to promote such knowledge, the idea emerged, under the influence of Darwin's theory of evolution and the Victorian idea of progress that the institutions of the non-European represented stages through which the European had passed long ago. This notion also gave a fillip to European Christian evangelism".[1]

Evolution was the idea that put into a coherent framework, the fast accumulating knowledge about the culture of the so-called primitives in various parts of the world.

Evolutionism, like it or not, seeks to explain the existence of the diversity of cultures, both in the past and in different places, by subsuming them under different phases in a single path of development; "it is really an attempt to wipe out the diversity of cultures while pretending to accord it full recognition. If the various conditions in which societies are found, both in the past and in the far distant lands, are treated as phases in stages in a single line of development, starting from the same point and leading to the same end, it seems clear that the diversity is merely apparent. Humanity is claimed to be one and the same everywhere but this unity and identity can be achieved only gradually : the variety of cultures we find in the world illustrates the several stages in a process which conceals the

# THE KHASI MILIEU

*Other Titles of Interest*

REKHA M. SHANGPLIANG
**Forest in the Life of Khasis**

MRINAL MIRI
**Linguistic Situation in North-East India**

---

**About the Author**

**H. Onderson Mawrie** is a major writer in Khasi. He is deeply committed to a serious articulation of the traditional Khasi world-view and religion and to freeing them from many errors of misinterpretation that they have suffered for long. His works in Khasi include Ka Pyrkhat U Khasi and U Khasi Bad la ka Niam.

**Sujata Miri** is currently Head of the Department of Philosophy at North-Eastern Hill University. She has been engaged, for several years now, in the study of tribal religion and culture. She is the editor of the book entitled Religion and Society of North Eastern India (Vikas, New Delhi). She is also the author of the book entitled: Suffering.

# THE KHASI MILIEU

**H.O. MAWRIE**

**Also**
An Introduction to the Study of Tribal Religions
*by*
**SUJATA MIRI**

CONCEPT PUBLISHING COMPANY PVT. LTD.
NEW DELHI-110059

**ISBN: 978-81-7022-181-4**

Edition 2026

*Published and Printed by*

Concept
Since 1974

**Concept Publishing Company Pvt. Ltd.**
A/15-16, Commercial Block, Mohan Garden,
New Delhi-110059 (India)
*T*: 91-11-41101460
*E*: publishing@conceptpub.com, *W*: www.conceptpub.com

# Preface

IT is generally claimed that tribal religions do not have any literature or tradition of interpretation which could articulate the significance of their religion in the life of the tribal people. This may generally be the case; but the Khasis are a remarkable exception to this rule, The oral literature of the Khasis, before it came to be written down, is amazingly rich in philosophical, theological and interpretative ideas concerning their religion.

The Seng Khasi organisation founded first on 23 August 1899, has been active in making this literature available to its members and others who are interested. Amongst the creative writings coming from this organisation, Mr. H. O. Mawrie's *Ka Pyrkhat U Khasi* deserves a special place. Though this book has been a prescribed text for the Bachelor's degree course in Khasi in Meghalaya, there has been no serious academic attempt to understand it. The purpose of publishing this translation is to try to stimulate academic discussion as well as to give it wider audience.

The translation work was part of a project I had undertaken with financial assistance from the Indian Council of Social Science Research. My thanks, therefore, are due to the Council for their generous assistance. Mr O. Wahlang did the major part of the translation for which I am extremely grateful to him. The North-Eastern Hill University has contributed generously towards the cost of publication of this book; my thanks are, therefore, due to the authorities of this University. I also acknowledge the help of Debjani Tarafdar, Querang Lungalang and Weidamon in preparing the munuscript.

SUJATA MIRI

## *A Note on H.O. Mawrie*

BAH Onderson's book on the Khasi concept of life is indeed a compact work of a genius. A long and tedious labour involving time in the search and research must have been passionately undergone by the author to have enabled him to produce such a concise, compact and incomparable piece of work. The various themes in the diverse chapters of this stupendous task could well serve as a foundation stone for dozens of volumes expanding the respective contents.

We have come across other accounts and expositions of the tenets of the Khasi race, Khasi culture and religion chiefly those by Dr. Homiwell Lyngdoh, U Rabon Singh, U Sib Charan Roy, U Jeebon Roy and Rev Fr G. Costa, but I think the author's present work surpasses all the preceding accounts. The author has great care and attention, with the aspiration to present the true picture of what exists in the original way of life, culture and religion of the Khasis as a race. Never a stranger to the Christian theology, Bah Onderson must have paid great attention to and made a thorough study of Comparative Religions, for him to stand back in awe and wonderment, when he is to discover his original religion—its meaning and its worth. Moulded in fundamentalism and tempered by bare circumstances of life itself, Bah Onderson Mawrie succeeds in transcending these, to bring light to others by creatively exposing the nature of Khasi life in its true perspection.

This book has turned to be a treasure house not only for the knowledge of the Khasi thought and his original way of life, but as a treatise to regain what is lost and retain and preserve what is still existing in our race. Reading it is a pilgrimage towards the real Khasi life, culture and religion.

Pohkseh, Shillong, — U OSCARD M. WAHLANG
the 9th October, 1980

# Contents

# *List of Plates*

# Introduction

THE EMERGENCE of history as the sovereign science of man exercised a tremendous influence on the anthropological study of religion. With it came an emphasis on the nature of primitive reasoning and the stages of its "evolution into civilized thought". While the intellectual tradition of the cultural evolutionists has been rejected in the west (specially with the advent of Freud and Durkheim), it is surprising to note that in much of Indian anthropology today there still persists the domination of the historicist's modes of thought in the understanding of culture and religion. This accounts for an unashamed, continuous description of tribal religions (including the Khasi religion) as spiritism or animism.

With the advent of science, educated Europeans began to account for their own religion as arising out of misunderstanding from false analogical reasoning and ignorance of natural causes. Accordingly, the religion of the uneducated and unscientific peoples appeared still more compounded of error and misunderstanding. The simplest form of religion, "animism", as Tylor had called it, arose so he thought, when primitive peoples had reflected upon their experience of immaterial forms in dreams or considered the difference between a living man and his corpse. Accordingly for him primitive religion was a means towards a knowledge and control of human circumstance and particularly of the physical world, which in his day men of science had really begun to achieve by rational methods.

Influenced by such an approach the early enquiries, mostly foreign, into Khasi religion oversimplified the problems of translation and interpretation of Khasi ideas and custom. Original writings culled from Khasi informants were very few. The scholars who claimed the Khasi mentality as a primitive mentality knew nothing of their language nor were they intimate with their social and cultural conditions. Consequently, Gourdon's interpretation, for instance, of Khasi religion remains the result of simple introspection. He is prepared (as other Victorian anthropologists) to compare as well as contrast 'savages' with him. For him the primitive gods of the Khasis were the product of more or less uninstructed human reason and imagination.

To Tylor the minimal definition of religion was "a belief in spiritual beings". Thus the understanding of religion came down to an understanding of the basis upon which such a belief arose at its most primitive level. Strangely enough, belief in spirits began as an uncritical effort to explain such puzzling phenomena as death, dreams and possession. Tylor believed that the idea of a soul was used to explain more and more remote and hitherto inexplicable natural occurrences until virtually every "tree and rock was haunted by some sort of gossamer presence". The "higher", more "developed" forms of "belief in spiritual beings", first polytheism, ultimately monotheism, were founded upon this animistic basis.

In official anthropology today, however, the term "animism" is firmly rejected, and this rejection is reflected even in elementary text-books on cultural anthropology. Thus, Melville J. Herskowits in his *Cultural Anthropology* p. 229, says :

> The term 'animism' cannot be applied to the total system of beliefs of any people. To characterise a religion in such terms is so broad as to be meaningless. Christianity is animistic in that the belief in the human soul is an integral part of it, but Christians do not officially believe that automobiles have spirits. On the other hand, a belief that a waterfall or a rock or a bear or mouse has a spirit does not necessarily exclude belief in pantheons of gods who direct the larger concerns of the universe, or in quite impersonal supernatural forces. Both these, in turn, can and in most instances do coexist, as part of the same system with ghosts and other manifestations of the spirits of the dead, perhaps formalized as an ancestral cult.

Wherever students have investigated the interrelations of their co-existing beliefs, they have found all such forms to be integrated into a unified world-view. This world-view, moreover, is not to be taken as evidence of a deficient or

> even a particular kind of mentality; it is the expression of a system of logic that moves with sureness from accepted premises concerning the nature of the world and man.

It is amazing, therefore, that writers on Khasi religion cannot till this day, shake off their fascination with the idea of "animism". The "experts" on Khasi religion claim the following :

> The religion of the Khasis may be described as animism or spirit worship, or rather, the propitiation of spirits both good and evil on certain occasions, principally in times of trouble. (Gourdon, *The Khasis*, 1907, p. 105)
>
> The religion of the Khasis is a rude animism or demon worship (*Census of India*, 1961, p. 86).
>
> A rather vague cult of the spirits supposed to live in trees, mountains, peaks etc. (Meerworth, *The Andamanese, Nicobarese and Hill Tribes of Assam*, 1919, Guide Book 2, p. 14).
>
> Khasi religion is demon worship or a jumble of enchantments muttered by priests who are sorcerers. (N. Natarajan, *TheMissionary among the Khasis*, 1977, p. 43).
>
> Khasi religion is both theistic and animistic. . .
> *History and Culture of the Khasi People*, 1967, p. 355 (H. Bareh).
>
> The original religion of the tribal people is what used to be called Animism . . . the contribution of a soul to natural phenomena.
> (*Hill India*, 1972, Vol. I, p. 326).
>
> The Khasi religion is both theistic and animistic though in the beginning it was apparently monotheistic.
> (K.L. Bhowmik, *Tribal India*, p. 126, 1971).
>
> Belief in the existence of spirits or deities which goes by the name of "animism" is not peculiar to the Khasis, nor does it make their religion particularly primitive.
> (J.N. Choudhury, *The Khasi Canvas*, 1978, p. 190-91).

The main reason for this, what I call 'animistic fixation', is undoubtedly the fact that writers on Khasi religion continue to be influenced by anthropologists like Lowie and Marshall and through them by Tylor. Tylor's influence is unmistakably present in Harry I. Marshall's study of the Karen people of Burma conducted in 1922 where he makes the following observations: "The second religious conception attained by the Karen was animistic. They entered upon this stage of religious belief when they began to assign personal attributes to the various powers about them, conceiving of every unknown force as a more or less distinct personality". Unfortunately, Marshall does not himself see the importance of his own observation about the Karen. "Every tree, river, lake and indeed, almost every natural object is supposed by the Karen to be inhabited by divinity". It is astounding how after making the above observation, the author reached the conclusion about the Karen by stating that the life of the Karen is therefore dominated by "superstitious beliefs in unseen and malicious powers".

Also, one might think in this connection of Lowie's study of Ekoi of Kamerun in Southern Nigeria. "A considerable portion of the Ekoi religion centres in the conception of ghosts and the ritual practice to avert or nullify their anger". At another place the same author observes "special locations are haunted by ghosts, among them two lakes shunned by the natives, who would not even track game in the vicinity for fear of arousing the vengeance of the snakes and crocodiles credited with the guardianship of these sacred waters. Ghosts are by no means all bad. The dominant note in the native attitude towards these spirits is fear. The Ekoi are afraid of the dark because they do not wish to encounter ghosts. Ghosts sometimes eat human beings. People take pains to exclude ghosts by wearing amulets or keeping lamps lit or by burning species; and they go to great trouble to conciliate them".

The same author talked about the Polynesian religion characterised as spiritism. On the one hand he declares "the entire fabric of the universe is constantly sustained by this 'Nangia' primary being". And this he cannot reconcile with the Polynesian conception of "the primeval gods numbering about 300". Among writers on tribal religions in India, Verrier Elwin is still among the most widely read. And the influence of Marshall and Lowie on his earlier writing is undeniable. Take, for instance, Elwin's study of the Soaras tribe of Orissa. His conclusion here is interestingly the same as that of Lowie's about Polynesian religion. On the one hand there is recognised

ultimate reality and delays our recognition of it".[2] Evolution is thus the refusal to accept the fact that the form and development of human life is not everywhere the same. But rather takes the form in an extraordinary diverse realm. Thus everything that does not conform to the evolutionist's system of criteria is either denied the name of culture where standards of values are involved, or are considered vague or unintelligible where it involves meaning and concepts. Such, perhaps, unintentional discrimination is to be found in P.R.T. Gourdon's *Reconstruction of Khasi Religion*, for example in his claim that "the Khasis have a vague belief in God". Discussing Khasi religion in Section 4 of his book, Gourdon makes the following two claims :

1. "The Khasis have a *vague belief* in God, the Creator".
2. "The Khasis cannot, however, be said to worship the Supreme God although it is true that they sometimes invoke Him when sacrificing and in times of trouble".

Let us examine the first of these claims. It may be that by the term "vague belief", Gourdon is describing his own state of unclarity about *U Blei.* While this is perfectly understandable, this is, of course not what he really means. The "vagueness" that he talks about is supposed to be part of the Khasi's idea of his God. But I think this is both misleading and potentially dangerous.

Without entering into the philosophical debate about vagueness of concepts I would like to make the following points about his notion :

(1) An idea might be vague *for* someone without being vague in itself. An idea may be vague for me in that I cannot spell out the conditions of its applications: but it need not follow from this that these cannot be spelt out at all. My idea of electron may be vague in this sense.

(2) On the other hand, there are concepts such that, from the nature of the case, the conditions of their application cannot be exhaustively spelt out. These are the

concepts to which Wittgenstein's idea of family resemblance has an application. Wittgenstein's multiple use of the concept of game as an illustration here is instructive. However, it does not at all follow from the family-resemblance idea that the concepts to which it applies are vague. There is no vagueness about the concept of game. It is clear as it can possibly be.

(3) A concept may be vague in itself in that any attempt to spell out the conditions of its application in detail inevitably leads to confusion or incoherence of one sort or another.

It may be thought that the notion of *U Blei* is vague in the sense of (3) above, indeed much philosophical criticism of religious ideas whether of Christianity, Buddhism or any other major religion of the world rests on the belief that they involve logical confusion of one sort or another. But such criticism is often inspired by a fairly arbitrary and mistaken assumption about the ultimate determinants of meaning. The philosophical debate concerning this also I shall pass by. I wish merely to make the remark that the clarity of a concept is sometimes a matter of its place in the total conceptual framework of a culture. When a concept plays a central role in the life of a culture, becoming clear about it coincides with the progressive exploration of this role.[3]

Such a central role is played by the concept of *U Blei* in Khasi religion. A reference to U Sib Charan Roy Jait Dkhar here would explain the concept of *U Blei.** Our forefathers attributed and explained that God is :

"God from above from below (Omnipresent) God, the Lord and Master, God, the Creator; and God, the Determiner of our life, the Dispenser; Oh God the Supreme power.

"This God is the only one God and there is no other God besides Him. He is Omniscient, Omnipotent and Omnipresent. He is the Lord of lords.

"As the Creator, He controls over man and all creatures. He gives a spirit to all living creatures. He works eternally.

* K[illegible] Niam Ki Khasi, Ka Niam Tip-Blei Tip-Briew, Ka 'Tien Hok' [illegible] Blei Don-Sot Dou-Kular.

> "As God is omnipresent, He is inside and outside of one's hearts. The Khasis offer a prayer to God because they know that God is with them and they are dependent on Him. The forefathers realised that God has given a spirit to all living creatures and has taught us that even the animals also have some spirit; since both man and animal have the same spirit, only talents and skills differ."

H. Onderson Mawrie in his article "God and Man" (published in the *Khasi Heritage*) writes the following : "God is the Creator of Man. We came into this world through that cause, out of that cause and by that cause. Man comes out of the righteousness of God and therefore he must act righteously, live righteously and earn that righteousness".

Gourdon's claim reflects the tendency of the evolutionists to take the part for the whole and the failure in his case to account for the place and role of *U Blei* which holds together in multifarious subtle ways, the entire network of meanings which constitute Khasi culture. It is of no wonder, therefore, that Gourdon found it vague for he considered it in isolation and so considered it is bound to appear truncated and strange. Moreover, the claim that since there are similarities between cultures there *must* be similarities in all respects between them is logically quite indefensible. It is also not surprising, therefore that Gourdon fails to establish the similarity in all respects between the Khasi *U Blei* and the Supreme God of his own culture and thereby concludes that the Khasi concept of *U Blei* is incoherent and vague. It is prima facie a denial of differences which he can no longer account for intellectually. But most importantly Gourdon's claim is also *dangerous* because it arises from the ego-centric view point of an alien imperial culture. This is a danger which anthropologists in spite of a great deal of talk about it have not really overcome as yet.

I have discussed Gourdon at some length, because his assumptions and framework continue to slip into studies of Khasi religion and culture, helped of course by the tacit acceptance by the latter of the muddled "anthropology of animism". In north-east India, this fact acquires special importance because there are powerful agencies whose very survival here depends primarily on the survival of evolutionary anthropology and the frame of mind which goes with it.

The name given to their religion by the Khasis is *Ka Niam Tip Briew Tip Blei*—the religion of knowing man, knowing God. There is no special means of knowing *U Blei*, knowledge of man and of God always go together.[4] Accordingly, what is important for a religious Khasi is not a commitment to a doctrine or dogma but his behaviour as man and how he conducts himself in his relation with other fellow human beings and to nature. His religion is therefore also characterised as *Ka Niam Ka Rukom* the religion of the correct observance of norms.

Knowledge of man consists fundamentally in the insight into the truth that, man must lead his life within a framework of rules and duties. It is important, in this connection, to note that the Khasi word for religion is derived from *Nia* which means reason. Religious knowledge is thus also the knowledge that man's life has a rational foundation which derives ultimately from *U Blei*.

Man is a creature of God. There is a covenant between God and man from the beginning of time. The Khasis begin their invocation with these words :

> God the Lord and Master, the one who assigns, the giver of Divine faith to us the Khasis, lo, I uphold the covenant between us from the beginning of creation. I am not like other races who seek you through written books or by bowing before idols and images.[5]

There are many parables about the creation of the universe and the relation between man and God.[6] Being all in all God is above gender, *U Blei*. In prayer they simply say *A Blei* or *Ka Blei* without using the masculine prefix *U* or the feminine prefix *Ka*.

The following are some of the things said about *U Blei* :

> **"U Blei is the name given to God. He is the Creator, Sustainer, all powerful, Omniscient and Omnipresent. Being all in all He is above gender and therefore the Khasi**

calls Him *U Blei.* God is the Creator of everything that has been, that is, and that will be.

"The Khasis believe that there is only one God who is the greatest Almighty. God is the Schemer and Creator (*U Nongbuh U Nong thaw*). He created the heaven and the earth and all things that are in heaven above and earth below. The Khasi regards God as Giver and Dispenser of life. God is the Supreme Being, all powerful and perfect". (H.O. Mawrie : *Ka Pyrkhat U Khasi*).

"The Khasis believe that God is Omnipotent, Omnipresent and Omniscient. Accordingly they hold it a sacrilege to symbolise God or to picture Him in any shape or form." (R.T. Rymbai : 'Some Aspects of the Religion of the Khasi Pnars" in *Khasi Heritage.*)

Since God is regarded as formless it is impossible adequately to symbolise Him by means of any spatio-temporal object; also it is improper to try to do so. Consonant with this idea, Khasis do not have temples, nor is there any iconographic tradition among them. *U Blei* is the unrepresentable source of everything but everything in the world bears the mark of His greatness. God the Creator of all fills the heaven and earth. God can be invoked anywhere and everywhere and with any names according to the need of the moment. There is no fixed day of congregational worship; "man must work to live and honest work is worship". He must be truthful in his thoughts and words and just in all his actions. The basic concept of Khasi religion is *Kamai Ka Hok* it means to "earn righteousness". Moreover, if a person lives a truthful and righteous life, after death his soul goes back to God and lives thenceforth in His presence. Hence, the Khasis call their dead *Bam Kwai h aing U Blei*—he who is eating betel nut in God's house. *U Blei* does not punish after death (there is no idea of hell) although the souls of those who have broken a taboo (*sang*) roam about the earth in various forms.[7]

As nothing material can be carried to the House of God, the emphasis is on earning righteousness, which is the only thing that can be associated with one forever. Hence living long in this world is a blessing as it offers a greater opportunity to earn righteousness.[8] Moreover, it is the individual alone who is responsible for his self-realisation, no other can achieve for him an entry into the House of God, accordingly there is no room for priesthood or sainthood.[9] However if misfortunes occur there are ways of finding out their causes. Nothing happens in the world without some cause and if a family or clan suffers from misfortunes of any kind, there are appropriate divinations aimed at finding out their cause. "The Khasi religion is usually known as 'religion of divinations', or that 'which involves primarily calculation and judgment', because in it consists man's urge to achieve what is good and righteous through the means of correct calculation and judgment, a calculation which cannot be wrong."[10] To account for any mishap the family resorts to divine consultation, they ask for the signs from grains of rice, *cowries* or other materials and should those not yield any result they use the egg-breaking or "cock-sacrificing" ritual. When they have discovered the cause, they perform sacrifices in atonement for their shortcomings in order that they may be freed from their afflictions etc., promising also to offer thanksgiving to God. In case they fail to discover the cause in spite of all their efforts the family takes the last resort of surrendering completely to God.

The worship of different deities like *U'lei Muluk*—the God of the State, *U' lei Shillong*—the God of Shillong peak, *U'lei Umtong*—the God of water, *U'Lei longspah*—the God of wealth, has been referred to as the polytheistic tendency of Khasi religion even by Khasi scholars like H. Bareh.[11] Here, I am afraid, I sense some error in interpretation.

In spite of propitiations to different deities (at various festivals) the theism is actually never abandoned. In Bareh's own words : ". . . the Supreme Being retains a predominant place in all cases of sacrifices. He or the supreme Goddess is first to be *invoked* and addressed before other spirits are to be appeased. His permission is first to be obtained by means of divination or otherwise". Again he admits "the Supreme Being is not altogether removed although the system becomes complicated and vague" (Shades of Gourdon?). Even Gourdon who describes the Khasi worship of gods and goddesses accepts a similar position. Note "They (i.e. the gods and goddesses) are even supposed to possess the power of life and death over man and woman, subject to the control of *U'Blei Nongthaw*, God the Creator.[12]

Granting the worship of sacred forests, rivers etc. the question is what is the relation between these "lesser or local gods" and *U'Blei*? The answer is easily found. They (i.e. the deities) of course "cannot be considered to be equivalent to the one God, the Creator, *U'Blei Uba ha jrong ha tbian* the God who is above and here below, is the God who is everywhere.[13] He is one although he can manifest Himself in different guises. Being omnipresent He gets temporarily identified with particular agencies. U Rabon Singh explains the above in the following manner "God manifests Himself in different places in a number of groves, forests, hillocks, peaks and rivers. For this reason, these places became places of worship".[14]

For Hamlet Bareh this becomes, in his words, "polluting animistic beliefs". According to Bareh the Khasi "animistic" rites consist mainly in the cult of fertility, worship of mountains and river spirits, divination, glorification of ancestress and other allied elements. The rites associated with cultivation in Jaintia and North Khasi Hills seem strange to the author, just as the recognition of forest groves and rivers as sacred, are proof of their primitiveness. So also offerings to the deceased ancestors whose assistance would aid the descendants to grow, thrive and prosper is enough reason for the critic to brand them as primitive because of their failure to differentiate the secular (dead bodies) from the sacred (the super-natural) Bareh's approach is consistent with the earlier approaches. One identifying feature of Khasi spiritism for the commentators is ancestor worship.

Here are six assertions from different authors:

(1) "The Khasis not only revere the memories of deceased ancestors but they adore them by means of offerings. These offerings take the shape of food . . . To honour a dead ancestor is the duty of every Khasi". (Gourdon)

(2) Gourdon also quotes U Hormu Rai Diengdoh "The real religious demand amongst the Khasis is the *ai bam* or giving food to the spirits of deceased ancestors . . . " (p. 110).

(3) "Every house has its little domestic shrine. The shrine

is one in which the ancestors are worshipped". (N.E. Bose, *Some Indian Tribes*, chap. "The Khasis" p. 156 published in 1972).

(4) "Ancestor worship is an important feature of the Khasi religion" (N. Natarajan: *The Missionary among the Khasis* p. 53, 1977).

(5) K. Chattopadhyay in *The Missionary among the Khasis* says, "Ancestor worship by offering food to the dead is an important ceremony . . . " (Published in 1978).

(6) "Ancestor worship plays an important part in Khasi religion". (P.R.G. Mathur, *Khasis of Meghalaya*, p. 62 Published in 1979).

What is of significance here is the fact that the offering of food to the dead ancestor, a rite commented upon by Hastings (in the *Encyclopaedia of Ethics and Religion*, Vol. I, p. 450), as "a rite common among all savages and semi-savage races", is recognised as yet another failure of the Khasis to recognise the sacred-secular dichotomy. The ancestors belong, let us say, to the secular world and only the supernatural or the other world or God is sacred. The critics fail to see that offerings are literally "not offerings to the ancestor but simply tokens of remembrance".[15] They (the offerings) are taken from the functional organs of the body to symbolise the continuity of life hereafter. There, unfortunately, also seems to be a determined effort not to heed the repeated denial by actual followers of the Khasi religion of the charge that "ancestor worship" in the form suggested by the critics is a feature of the Khasi religion (R.T. Rymbai and others).

The point I wish to emphasise in this connection is that within a religious world view any one aspect of creation may be chosen for special religious attention; nor does this rule out the possibility of there existing more than one symbol of divinity.

There are places within the Khasi and Jaintia Hills which are accorded special religious significance. They have—in relation to other places—acquired greater symbolic power, and this power is partly embodied in "legends" associated with them. Take the legend associated with the city of Shillong. In the ancient days both the Khasis and the Syntengs claimed that the Shillong God belonged to them. To settle this dispute it was decided to inquire from *U'lei Shillong* Himself whose God, whether of the Khasis' or the Jaintias', He was. On a fixed day both the parties appeared at a particular spot and the Khasis requested one member of the Synteng to speak to God first. *Me te U Blei jong i me*? (Art thou our God?), said the Synteng. No answer came in reply. However, when a Khasi asked the same question of God, the answer came "Yes" three times. From that day onwards the Syntengs ceased to claim the city of Shillong.[16] Also there is a myth about how the Shillong God saved the Khasis from the Japanese aeroplanes by causing a horrible and tremendous storm to blow over the hills.

The Khasi religion is quite explicit in its assertion that there can be no sphere of human life on which religion does not have a crucial bearing.

God has brought every man into existence with reason and design and He expects man to uphold his reason (*Ka Rngiew*) at all times. He has also placed him in a family as well as a clan. Hence, He lives in the world not alone but with the God of the clan (*Ka Blei*), the Ancestress (*Ka Inwbei*), the Ancestor (*U Thawlang*) and the Uncle (*U Suidnia*), who all compose the *dawiing*. It is impossible to isolate a man's responsibility to himself from a man's responsibility to his family and clan. Whatever man does he is aware that by his doings (good or bad) he commits not only himself but also his family and clan to the consequences of his actions.

A look at the traditional Khasi idea of the "true" significance of marriage will make this clear. Marriage is something more than a union of two individuals or even their immediate families. It involves a relationship between whole groups of people; the proposal for marriage comes from the groom's side through his mother or aunt, with the approval of his maternal uncle, after it has been established that there is no kinship between the couple or the families forbidden by custom and religion. The couple is joined in wedlock by a ceremony performed in the girl's house after dusk. After sunset the girl's maternal uncle and other friends and relatives go to the boy's house to fetch him. The boy is accompanied by his maternal uncle along with friends and relatives.[17] The marriage ceremony is conducted by the two maternal uncles. At the time of the marriage the priest abjures *U'Blei* in the following manner:

Hei oh God from above: oh God from below;
Oh *Lei Synshar*.
Oh God who has created man:
As Thou hast ordained this marriage . . . .
Thou wilt bless them;
Thou will grant them prosperity;
Thou wilt show them the way; . . . . .[18]

The violation of an established rule of conduct is considered *Ka Sang ka pap*. The following are a few of the taboos and the consequences resulting from their violation:

| *Ka Sang* | *Consequences* |
|---|---|
| 1. Marriage within the same clan<br>2. Marriage with the father's brother.<br>3. Marriage with the sister's cousin or aunt of the father | Excommunication from the entire society and prohibition from participation in ritual performance. |
| 4. Witchcraft<br>5. Adultery | Exile from the village. Birth of deformed or otherwise abnormal children. |
| 6. Suicide<br>7. A Khatduh who gets converted to Christianity | Prohibition from participation in ritual and deprivation of inheritance. |
| 8. To murder a fellow human being[19] | Excommunication from the clan. |

The commission of *Ka sang* 1, 2 and 3 is considered unpardonable, debarring offenders from all rights and privileges vouchsafed by custom. So also the violation of 5, 6 and 8 necessarily entails banishment and complete rejection of the culprit as a respectable member of the community. In case of ***Ka Sang*** 7 in recent times a concession is made in the sense that if a *Khatduh* renounces Christianity she will be accepted back in the clan and can claim all her rights. What I wish to stress here is that undoubtedly *Ka Sang* promotes the maintenance of social and natural order *but* it does not do so in abstraction from the religious order. This social order is neither separated nor separable from the religious order. Actually we can, in a certain sense, go so far as to claim that the two are one and the same. If an offender threatens the stability of the society even God cannot protect him (*Ka Sang* 1, 2 and 3). Religious rituals are interwoven with social norms and the greatest punishment is excommunication from the clan and not merely burning in hell in a life hereafter.

Two notions which man be said to be basic in the Khasi conception of his society are those of *Kur* and *Kha*. All those who have descended from the same ancestral mother belong to the same *Kur*.* Members of other *Kurs* are *Kha*. As the Khasis are descendants of the ancestress goddess an important status is assigned to women by the Khasis. Accordingly it is the *Khatduh* (Youngest daughter) who inherits the lion's share of the mother's property. But demands on her are enormous in keeping with religion. She is literally the keeper of *Niam* (religion) and her house is calld *Ka iingseng*. Here all the family assemble to witness her perform all rites and rituals. She cremates her mother, puts the bones of all the members of the family in their final resting place (*Maw Bah* or clan cairn) and if any member of the family is unable to support himself or herself he or she has the right to being fed at the *iing Khatduh*.

Certain evolutionist ideas about matriliny—now widely rejected in professional circles—seem, perhaps not surprisingly, still to vitiate ordinary thinking about Khasi society. These are ideas such as the following :

(a) matrilineal peoples are primitive "promiscuous hordes" and therefore (b) their children would necessarily be brought up by only their mothers, the particular father being unknown to them. "There is no historical evidence for this argument, and it will certainly not hold if the supposedly more 'primitive' matrilineal descent is assumed to be associated with a general cultural poverty and simplicity. The matrilineal Nayar, or matrilineal peoples like the Akan of China, Minan or Kaban of Sumatra and even the plains Indians of North-America are by any standards as highly organised socially as many patrilineal peoples and culturally far richer than some". (Godfrey Lionhardt, *Social Anthropology*, p. 119m).

The members of the same Kur no matter how far removed cannot inter-marry. Marriage is strictly outside the Kurs. There cannot be a greater sin (*Ka sang*) than a union between members of the same clan. The society places the demands of kinship as above the rule of the state and as at par with religious precepts. In traditional Khasi society there are other similar rules of conduct the violation of which is threatened with social boycott or banishment or deprivation of some kind *outside the domain of law*. However, in most of contemporary Khasi society this is not quite the case. There is a change in that, for reasons into which I do not wish to enter here, there has come about a rift between the social and the religious. My point can be illustrated with reference to *Ka sang*. Earlier the youngest daughter, if converted to Christianity, was deprived of her inheritance rights along with prohibition from participation in religious functions. However, today, the *Ka sang* connected with this is overlooked for social and legal purposes, although the performance by her, of the traditional religious rites and practices is still prohibited. In other words, today her social and political status is divorced from and is independent of her religious identity.

Unlike the societies which have come under the sway of historical religions, in traditional Khasi society there is a single religio-political hierarchy. The "secular" and religious leadership are combined in one person, i.e. the Syiem. But the important point to note is that though there is leadership in the traditional society yet the pattern of election is democratic. The Syiem who is the chief or head of the village is elected by the people. To check the misuse of power by him and to also help him in matters of administration there are myntries, basans lyngshkor etc., who in their turn are also elected from different clans.

The democratic way of life of the Khasis is well depicted in the Nongkrem Dance, the annual religious ceremony of the Khyrim Syiemship. The state of which the Syiem is the head is composed of Raids or different groups of villages. These Raids in token of friendship and loyalty bring sacrificial goats to the Syiem during the festival without any special distinction at all. All pray together to God to give them strength and wisdom and to promote happy understanding between the ruler and the ruled.

The different clans have their own elected headman (who is elected from amongst the males of the clan). Each family within the clan manages its own internal affairs under the supervision of its elders. However, the final say lies in the jurisdiction of their headman who not only settles legal disputes but also conducts rituals and ceremonies on behalf of the clan assisted by his maternal relatives and clan elders.

To settle disputes involving crimiual offences the Durbar is proclaimed by the Syiem who acts as the judge. Both sides have their own pleaders and the hearing commences only after due prayers to the goddess of the state or *Ka 'lei Synshar*. Over the Syiem and his Durbar of myntries, lyngskhors, basans and lyngdohs there is a higher authority which is supreme called *Durbar Bima* (State Assembly). It is also called *Ka Durbar Blei* (the Assembly of God). Hence its authority is final and its sanctity divine. It alone can decide important issues like de-throning of a Syiem or selecting of a new ruler. To ensure maturity in thought and debate, the representatives who are to attend the Durbar are all above 50 years of age.

The British Government effected drastic changes in the powers and functions of the Syiem.[20] After subjugation by the British they lost their age-old freedom of dispensation of justice among their people. For instance the Syiem and his officers in the twenty five states in the Khasi Hills were allowed the exercise of their traditional power to try only mild civil and criminal cases. But serious crimes like murder, homicide and accidental death were all referred to the Deputy Commissioner for his verdict.

Immediately after independence the Khasi Syiems revived the Khasi State Federation (which had been originally formed in 1934) for the administration and dispensation of justice. But after the formation of the District Council (in 1952) once again some of the powers enjoyed by the Federation were curtailed, and eventually it led to the emergence of a new pattern of leadership among the Khasis. Thus the Syiem who was the guardian of Khasi law and of moral authority, the protector of his people during times of war and peace is today reduced to being merely a Syiem in name, that also for presiding over certain religious ceremonies. Today the Khasis are ruled by the Meghalaya State officials and District Councils.

The main occupation of the people was cultivation, agricultural products being mainly paddy, rice, potato, betel nut and betel leaf. This again was regarded as something God-given, God in his mercy gave the inhabitants of the Seven Huts the gift to till the land and to produce food. Hence it is not becoming to disturb or obstruct anyone at work. "Should one need another's tools or implements in one's work one should ask for permission before using the tools and take special care of them while in use and return the same in a courteous way".[21]

Moreover in case there is a widow or a self-supporting female member in a village it is the duty of the entire village particularly of the youth to help her. At least one adult member from each household is required to jointly bear her burden in the cultivation of her fields. In case she is reduced to starvation and begging it will be a matter of shame for her entire village community.

On the arrival of the sowing and harvesting seasons all strong adults do community service. They form voluntary groups and help one by one each family of the neighbourhood by working in their fields till dusk. The household in turn provides free morning and evening meals for them.

So also the male youth offer to care for and nurse the sick at night. In case of death it becomes the duty of the entire village to help in the disposal of the dead body with due ceremony and observance of ritual.

Like in most modern societies, the sacred/secular dichotomy has also invaded Khasi-Jaintia society. Take the role of the Seng Khasi organisation. The aim of this organisation was set forth as that of safeguarding the truths of Khasi doctrines of religion and custom from the onslaught of alien influences.

The organisation adopted the following four principles with a view to implementing its objectives :

(1) Adherence to the tenets of kinship as specified by the ancestors.
(2) Righteousness through service, love and truth and a desire to improve both mind and body.
(3) Respect for one's own fellowmen and cultivation of humility.
(4) To work for one's country with faith in God.

Leading intellectuals of this organisation, like Maham Singh, A.S. Khongphai, Hipshon Roy, Kynpham Singh and R.T. Rymbai, are all involved in bringing out publications and organising discussions highlighting the importance of preserving the Khasi heritage. However, the larger part of the activities of the organisation is restricted to the organisation of symbolic traditional dances like *Shad Suk Mynsiem* (Thanksgiving Dance) or the Nongkrem Dance, activities which may be considered to be non-controversial, not demanding a total commitment of thought, deed and action involving political economical and social goals. This demonstrates the erosion of the truly tribal (religious) character of our tribal societies.

In Khasi culture there are enough examples to show how divine sanctions are sought to enforce their social and political order. A functionalist would find fairly convincing explanation for the divinisation of social labours. Let me illustrate this with an example. The Khasi had sacred groves of forests at the outskirts of almost every village. It was considered *sang* or taboo to cut live wood from those forests for it was held that God would wring the neck of any offender. However, there was no harm if any villager removed dead wood for domestic use. There could hardly be a better policy for the preservation of forests in any tradition. However, I am far from suggesting that one can give an exhaustive account of Khasi or any religion in functionalist terms alone. I have already argued to some extent against that earlier. Functionalism amounts to reductionism. While religious activities undeniably have a functional role—whether social, psychological or political—their meaning transcends the boundary of any such role. And it is characteristic of religious meaning that it necessarily binds together in one whole, of course in an inevitably oblique and complex manner, man, nature and the transcendent world. My plea is that instead of looking at Khasi religion (or any tribal religion) as a collection of more or less disconnected activities with more or less disparate areas of human life, we should consider it as a system of meanings with its centre in the concept of *U Blei*. This concept as it were, breathes life into the entire range of activities. I would here agree with Ninian Smart when he says "one requires in one's phenomenology an interactionism in which the gods themselves are members of the wider society under consideration".[22] I wish only to add that it is the pervasive membership of *U Blei* in this society that makes the most crucial difference in their phenomenology.

## REFERENCES


1. P. 180, *Sociological Bulletin*, Volume 22, No. 2, September 1973, article—"The development of sociology and social anthropology in India" by M.N. Srinivas and M.N. Panini. According to Srinivas and Panini, "the All India Census first undertaken in 1871 by the British also became an instrument of the official policy. Sir Herbert Risley, Commissioner of the 1901 Census for instance noted as well as deplored the tendency of the tribes to become Jatis which meant their absorption into Hinduism. In observations such as this can be seen the germs of the policy of erecting barriers between Hindus and the other groups and sections".
2. Claude Lévi-Strauss "Race and History", Published in the book *Race, Science and Society*, ed. by Leo Kuper, p. 102, first published in 1973.
3. Also compare N. Smart : "the full existence claim is unnecessary to the depiction of their powerful reality to the participants". (p. 73. *The Science of Religion* and *The Sociology of Religion*).
4. "Man-knowing and God-knowing go hand in hand. To know oneself is to know God because the self is the reflecting mirror of God. Again God is within all human beings, when we love human beings, we love God.' (H.O. Mawrie : *U Khasi bad Ka Niam*).
5. *Religion and Society of North-East India*, p. 45.
6. *H.O. Mawrie* : *Ka Pyrkhat U Khasi*, Chap. 3, *U Khasi Bad Ka Niam*.
7. There is a popular belief that those who have not lived righteously will go to *Khyndai Pateng Niamra—Nurok Ka Ksew*, the ninth chamber under the surface of the earth, where only dogs will walk. Lyngdoh refers to it as the kingdom of *U Jom* (courtesy Kelian Synrem).
8. For moral commandments see : *Ka Niam Ki Khasi* by U Sib Charan Roy Jait Dkhar.
9. In recent discussions with informers one did hear of exceptional cases of individuals claiming 'possession by God' in almost epileptic type of fits. But such instances are rare and do not get the attention or admiration of clan members.
10. U Rabon Singh, *Ka Kitab Niam—Khein Ki Khasi*.
11. See *Meghalaya Religious Belief and Ritual*.
12. P.R.T. Gourdon, *The Khasis*, p. 116.
13. (Courtesy Sitimon Sawian and Brandon M. Pugh).
14. Ka Kitab Niam Khein Ki Khasi, p. 11.
15. Kynpham Singh, *Khasi Heritage*, p. 100, published in 1979
16. There is a feeling that the Khasis had cheated the Jaintia by keeping a man hidden in a trench who spoke instead of God (courtesy Motiferr Rani)

17. R.T. Rymbai, *Khasi Heritage*, p. 77-78.
18. Refer U Jeebon Roy's notes o~ Khasi Religion. Also quoted in Gourdon's *The Khasis* and Lyngdo... s book.
19. Even the killing generally justified during war time is to be remedied with ritual observances.
20. Syiemship was accepted by the Khasis to be an institution of divine origin and was accordingly styled as *Ki Syiem U Blei.*
21. H.O. Mawrie, Chapter 11, "A Khasi bad Ka Akor" in *Ka Pyrkaat U Khasi.*
22. See *The Science of Religion* and *The Sociology of Religion* by Ninian Smart.

# 1

# *Man*

IN MANY religions of the world, the idea of the genesis of man is not very clear. Hinduism, Buddhism and Jainism, the three religions which originated in India, do speak about the rebirth of man but there is no clear conception of man prior to his birth. The Jews, on the other hand, believe that a man is the creature of God. It is God who made human beings and also the heaven and the earth and all things in the sky high above and on the earth down below. The Khasi concept of man is similar to that of the Jews. A Khasi believes that God made him, which means that He made him a full-fledged man to inhabit this world. A man belongs to God during his life time as well as when he has left this world. After he leaves this world he goes to "God's house" to spend his time chewing betel (*bam kwai ha iing U Blei*). The body will decay and perish but the soul belongs to God and to Him shall it return.

The Khasi thinks that man is a special creature of God. He is incomparably higher than any other creature. Man alone can express his mind and commune with God. If there is any deterioration on his part as a man, it is either because he does not submit himself before God or because he forsakes Him altogether. If there is any deterioration of his race it is also because the race does not abide by or fulfil the Commandment of God.

Whenever a Khasi prays he utters the following words :

> Oh God! Lord of all, Thou Creator and Maker of all things, Thou Giver of our breath, Who hath bestowed upon us the divine life and the capacity to grow in stature, with two-folded hands we beseech Thee, we submit.........

Man's capacity to grow morally and spiritually is quite special to him—and this is God's particular gift to man: the element of the divine in man. If there is any deterioration or decay in man's divine life, man himself is responsible for that. A Khasi speaks of that epoch when man lived by the side of God and God walked hand in hand with him talking to him face to face. That epoch was the golden age when justice and righteousness reigned supreme and it was the world at the beginning of time, before the darkness of *Ka Krem Lamet Ka Krem Latang* enveloped this world. Though this golden age has passed, yet it is the soul of this age that holds fast and moulds the Khasi religion and the relationship of a Khasi with his God.

A Khasi says that it is God who gave man his capacity to grow in stature. This idea of "growth in stature" (*Ka Longrynieng Ka Manrynieng*) to a Khasi, has a wide connotation. It includes the growth of the different dimensions of his personality and that of his unique intelligence. Other creatures are devoid of such capacity for growth.

Another divine gift to man, a Khasi believes, is the unique gift of *Ka Rngiew*. *Ka Rngiew* is man's capacity to bring rational considerations to bear upon his understanding of his own situation. When man has lost this capacity (*Ka Rngiew*), he has lost the very being of his life. A man who has lost this "spiritual amulet", is reduced virtually to a lower species of creation "like an insect or a bird". Even his good fortune and material success in life desert him when he has bad *Ka Rngiew*. In this case, it is said that the *Ka Rngiew* of a man has fled to the devils or to other evil powers, and the real cause of it is that man has gone astray from God, and so God must forsake him. No other power in this world can restore to man his lost *Ka Rngiew* except his own sincere endeavour towards peace with God.

A man, who has gone astray, has turned away from God's Commandment and Judgement (*Ka Hukum ka Bishar*)—and once entangled in this situation, other powers can easily rob him of whatever *Ka Rngiew* might be left in him. Once he is deprived of this divine gift, his personality and intelligence are on the wane. To regain them he has to perform the ceremony of *tap-Rngiew* or *Ksan Rngiew*. He must pray and invoke the blessings and forgiveness of God, find out for himself (with the help, perhaps, of divination) the cause of his loss of *Ka Rngiew* and perform the necessary sacrifices to pacify and satisfy God. Should the cause lie, for instance, in some transgression of the sanctity of the family (*Dawiing Dawsem*) for which God had to abandon a man to the mercy of the evil spirits, it is for the man himself to devise ways and means to regain his lost gift so that he might again be able to raise his head high as a human being.

The Khasi believes that this world is full of the powers of darkness and evil and that the sole function of these powers is to dislodge man from his place given to him by God. Man cannot fight these powers on his own. His strength lies in the "presence of God" in him and therefore, God, must always remain in the resolve of his heart. The man of God and prayer knows that the strength God has bestowed upon him is adequate for him in his battle against any power in this world. He therefore lives with constant confidence in God unshaken in his knowledge that God shall never desert him so long as he keeps the covenant with Him.

Man also realises that his life here in this world is but a short and temporary sojourn and this world is but an inn. To him God, who is righteous, also demands righteousness from man and therefore his duty is to earn righteousness. Throughout his life he strives to attain that goal. He also realises that as a man he is not perfect and commits many mistakes of omission and commission; therefore he asks for forgiveness from God for such acts. When he knows that God is offended, he devotes himself relentlessly in prayer and submission and when he can no longer sustain himself he surrenders himself entirely to God with the faith and hope that God will spare him. He satisfies himself by concluding his prayer with, "As Ye, God, will have it".

# 2

# God

THE TRADITION of theological thinking among the Khasi is perhaps the finest of all their traditions. "Theology" is a Greek word. "Theo" means "God" and "logy" means "wisdom". So, "theology" means "the wisdom or knowledge about God". The Khasis have certainly shown as much subtlety and profundity in their theological thinking as any other people in the world.

The Khasis, like the Jews, never seek to formulate arguments to prove that God exists. They take it for granted that God exists and that there is only one God who is omnipresent, omnipotent and eternal. Much as the Jews believe that God has revealed Himself to Abraham, Jacob, Moses and to others, a Khasi also believes that God reveals Himself to man. The God of a Khasi is not blind, neither is he deaf or dumb, since a blind, a deaf and a dumb being can in no way "introduce" himself. Without this introduction or revelation we will never be able to know what kind of a being God is.

God may reveal Himself to man in any or all of the following ways :

(i) through His power,
(ii) through His righteousness, and
(iii) through His spoken word.

To a Khasi God reveals Himself through nature and the world He has made. The beauty and splendour of nature and this world that God has made, the broad expanse and greatness of the universe with the sun and the moon and the myriad stars on the firmament, so regulated in their respective courses—all these speak of the wisdom of God—the wisdom that ever pervades His thought at all times. To a Khasi it is only the unimaginably great mind of an omnipotent God that could create and sustain the wonderful harmony of such things as these in heaven and on earth.

God, to a Khasi, is righteousness itself. And he reveals righteousness to man. Man partakes of this divine righteousness that is revealed to him; and when this happens, an egg will not break even though it is thrown with great force against the *diengshat* (a piece of wood used in Khasi divination where egg-breaking is done). Similarly when such a man catches hold of a flaming torch the fire will not burn; nor will a red hot piece of iron do any harm when it touches his flesh. It is this divine righteousness that guides man.

A Khasi believes that God reveals Himself to man through the spoken word, and the communication is through signs only after the days of *Ka Krem Lamet Ka Krem Latang*. When a man wants to know the will of God or wants to hear God's decree he makes a divine consultation through the medium of an egg or a fowl or any other animal judging the divine response from the signs that he asks for, or submits before God. Before any important event in a Khasi's life, divine consent or guidance is sought.

The words Jehovah of the Jews, Allah of the Muslims and God in English means *U Blei* in the Khasi language. It is interesting to note that all these words are in the masculine gender. But to a Khasi the name God is above the rules of gender and the question of determining the masculinity or feminity of God cannot possibly arise. He is the alpha and omega: He is omnipotent, He is omnipresent. From Him emerge the beginning of all things and in Him lies the ending of all things. Therefore, whether we call *U Blei* (masculine) or *Ka Blei* (feminine) it makes the same sense.

The Jews, the Muslims and the Christians maintain that there is only one God and the Khasis also maintain that there is only one God who is the greatest, "Almighty". But when a Khasi occasionally speaks of "the gods" (*ki Blei*), this must not be taken to mean that for him there is more than one

God. Khasis are not polytheists. Occasionally, talk of many gods is rather to be understood as talk about the multiplicity of the manifestations of one and the same God. To a Khasi God is one and many because of his attribute of being present in all the world above and the earth below.

To a Khasi, God is the supreme Planner and Creator (*U Nongbuh u Nongthaw*). One of the peoples that define God as the Creator is the Jewish people. In the book of Genesis of the Bible we find God defined as the Creator. He created the heavens and the earth and all things thereon and last of all he made man. To a Khasi it is not just that. To a Khasi God made all His plans beforehand and then set out to create. For this reason the word *Nongbuh* (planned) precedes the word *Nongthaw* (Creator). Before God created, he made, as it were, a "scenario" of the world where everything fitted into the whole. Everything had its proper place and order in this "scenario". This is why there is unchallengeable harmony in this world.

Creation is only the beginning; God also guarantees the continuity of what He has created. It is here that a Khasi regards God as *U Nongsei U Nongpynlong* (Giver and Dispenser of Life). A withered tree blooms forth to life again according to the scheme and the arrangement of God (the Giver and Dispenser of Life). With the giving of life and dispensation of the same, the creative process continues and thus it is that God as the Creator lives forever and His power rules eternally.

In His relationship with man, God again assumes the attribute of *U Nongthaw-bynriew U Nongbuh-bynriew*—(Creator of mankind and Planner of mankind). In this aspect we see that the word *Nongbuh* (Planner) succeeds the word *Nongthaw* (Creator). It is so as it befits God to "create" the Universe after he has "planned" the entire "creation" in proper order. But man being the crown of His creation, he must have a constant and special relationship with the Creator, mankind therefore needs a special plan to regulate his (man's) peace and harmony with God. It is this solemn relationship between man and God and all other things which binds man within the covenant which becomes God's commandment to him. In this aspect God to a Khasi becomes *Nonghukum bad Ka Nongshyn-*

*shar* (The Supreme Commander and Ruler) who disposes the lot of mankind throughout the length and breadth of the world.

A Khasi addresses God with diverse names but all these names are only to express the qualities and attributes relating to different functions of God in His particular relation to man. The names indicated above, namely *U Nongbuh U Nongthaw* (Planner and Creator), *U Nongsei U Nongpynlong* (Giver and Dispenser of Life) and *U Nongthaw-bynriew U Nongbuh-bynriew* (Creator of mankind and Architect of mankind) refer particularly to God in His capacity as the Creator of the world and man. As mentioned above another name attributed to God is *Ka Nongsynshar bad ka Nonghukum* (the Ruler and Supreme Commander). Sometimes He is also called *Ka Hukum* (the Command) as He is the Supreme embodiment of the authority vested in the *Jutang* (covenant). The covenant enjoins that righteousness stands upright and man keeps himself away from sacrilegious acts as well as from profane deeds or performances that may turn against the doer. This will keep a man whole and save him from straying from good in this world. It is God as *Ka Nongsynshar* (the Ruler) who will reward man according to his deeds and who will award punishment by delivering him to the devil when he ignores or forgets the covenant and violates the commandments.

Another name by which a Khasi addresses God is *U Blei-long-spah* (god of wealth), and this name was given because od's commandment and support extend over man's economic activity just as they do over any other activity of his. This ensures that a man's personal or his family's contribution to the clan's purse will be substantial. Still another name by which God is known is *Ka 'Leilongkur* (God of the clan). When God created mankind, He grouped different families and clans each belonging to a different ancestress who owns a separate stone cairn where the bones of all the clanmen were interned under one ancestral maternal uncle (*U Suidnia*). It is God as *'Leilongkur* that looks after the well-being of the clan as a whole. This *'Leilongkur* or *'Leilogjaid* goes hand in hand with the *lawbei* or ancestress and those two figure simultaneously in rituals connected with sacrifice or performance of rites pertaining to the clan. This *'Leilongkur* or *'Leilongjald* is commonly termed as *Ka Blei* (the Godhead) and an egg-breaking ritual is usually performed to consult or find out (in the course of communication with God), if there is any displeasure on the part of the Godhead and the Ancestress. When a sacrifice for a sick person is done with a cock-sacrifying ritual, after ripping open the intestines of the cock to find out the answer, the performer says, "Say ye oh God, the indisposition that is mine, the thrashes that are mine. . . . .". When he has found out the cause and when he says his grace on the recovery of the patient with, "Do hear, do listen to me ye Godhead and Ancestress, now when I have found the way out of my sheer failure. . . . ." and so on and so forth.

Other names a Khasi uses to address God are *U 'Leimuluk u 'Leijaka* (God of territory) and similarly *U 'Leikhyrdop u 'Leikharai* (God of war) to guard the gates and trenches at times of war with outsiders. In ancient days the Khasi menfolk were seldom found in their village. After they had established their kingdom on these Khasi Hills they used to invade the surrounding plain areas to expand the territory of their kingdom. In their own hill abode they used to build villages and hamlets, and also to fortify their defence they used to build strong ramparts, entry gates and also dug wide and deep trenches around those establishments. Victorious from their wars, they would return home joyous and happy chanting their usual battle rhymes. They used to perform befitting rituals to offer thanksgiving to *U 'Leimuluk u 'Leijaka* and *U 'Leikhyrdop u 'Leikharai*. The Khasi males in ancient times were soldiers or warriors by training and therefore they were fond of calling themselves by names such as *Ki Khla Ka Wait*, *Ki Khyndnai-bah Ryntich* depicting heroism in battles. Before they set out on a war expedition they would invoke the blessings and assistance of God and on return they would bow down in thanks giving to Him as *U 'Leimuluk u Leijaka*.

There are still other names that a Khasi gives to God and as pointed out before, the names refer to different important functions of God. In short, a Khasi believes that God is the Supreme Being, all-powerful and perfect. He is not stern nor wrathful, nor is He jealous and vengeful on His people. He is full of love and mercy. When a Khasi suffers any affliction, He performs his rituals with the aid of *Ka Shanam*, cowries, rice grains, an egg or a hen to find out the cause of the affliction and submits himself to God in prayer for his recovery. When he fails to find the cause, and all his trials fail, then he completely surrenders himself to God and His mercy, with the submission, "As You will have it, oh God". After this submission, come what may, he is reconciled and he takes it that God's will is done. This mode of thinking of a Khasi emanates from his complete trust upon and instinctive devotion to God.

# 3

# *Religion*

FOR a Khasi *Ka Niam* (religion) necessarily complements *Ka Rukom* (rite); hence the phrase *Ka Niam Ka Rukom. Ka Rukom* indicates the ceremonial aspect of religious observances, which must be according to the norms laid down in *Ka Niam*. The observances may occur in diverse ways and may differ from one part of the land to another but the principles of *Ka Niam* are the same. Observances and practices may differ even from one family to another but such diversity does not affect the religion.

To understand religion a spiritual development is necessary. It is so because all religions are based on faith. Religious truths are also conveyed through parables and mysterious words and to understand these we also need the inspiration of God and the power of faith. For instance, to understand about God's creation of this universe as was written in the book of Genesis of the Bible, or the mystery of the Garden of Eden itself, it needs faith and spiritual power. Similar is the case with the Khasi religion. As is the case with the creation of the universe or the Garden of Eden, so is the case with the *Aiom Ksiar* (Golden Age) when God was walking hand in hand with man, or with *Ka Krem Lamet Ka Krem Latang.*

The Khasi religion illustrates the relationship between man and God through parables and mysterious words. Once upon a time, when righteousness prevailed throughout mankind, there was a tree which served as a ladder to *Ki Khathynriew Trep ki Khathynriew Skum* (the Sixteen Families) for their communication between heaven and earth. This tree grew on top of *U Lum Sohpetbneng* (the Navel Peak of Heaven) which is the centre of the world. This tree formed the golden bridge ensuring physical contact between man and God till the time when transgression became the order of the day and this bridge gave way—thus destroying the communicating link between heaven and earth.

The parable of *Ka Krem Lamet Ka Krem Latang* is about sin. The story is as follows: Once upon a time when all the creatures in this world were honest and had only one language among them, a thanksgiving dance was arranged. Each and every creature came to participate in the dance, dressed in gorgeous attire to befit the occasion. The dance continued for the whole day and by late afternoon the crowd began to disperse. Just then, the Sun and the Moon, a sister and brother, arrived on the scene to participate in the dance. There was really nothing wrong with their steps but in spite of that there was a great uproar of scornful laughter on the ground that they being sister and brother were dancing together. This laughter of insult arose not because there was anything peculiar in their dance but because sin had taken root in the heart of mankind and man saw evil where there was none. Shame betook the Sun who fled away to *Ka Krem Lamet Ka Krem Latang* and immediately complete darkness enveloped the earth. The meaning of the story is clear. Darkness came not because the Sun had hidden inside the *Krem Lamet Krem Latang* but because sin had found its way among mankind and the power of darkness had won over the power of light.

There are no darker days to the Khasi to match the days of *Ka Krem Lamet Ka Krem Latang.* In this parable the Khasi realise that sin has overtaken them, righteousness has stepped aside and it is the end of the golden age. Terrible times are coming and man is at his wit's end. He gropes in the dark and the powers of darkness gain the upper hand over him. He understands that the time has come for him to turn his soul to God and he is confident that God will readily hear him should he bow down and devote himself to God and also that God would receive him. It is man's return to, and reconciliation with God which is the beginning of religion. The ritual of offering birds or animals in a sacrifice is a fact and experience, known and practised the world over and it is nothing strange then, that it is also prevalent in the Khasi religion. There is no problem in understanding it. What is more difficult to grasp is its basis in Khasi philosophy.

According to the Khasi, religion is the relationship between man and God and this relationship is governed by two factors, namely, *Ka Nia* and *Ka Jutang* (reason and covenant). The principal reason for man is that he is a creature of God. Man belongs to God during his lifetime as well as after he has left this world. His permanent habitation is with God. The covenant on the other hand is that as long as man is alive in this world he should abide by and execute the command (*hukum*) of God by earning righteousness—and on God's part the covenant is that God shall take care of man.

A Khasi understands that there is no covenant that can be executed by only one party. The covenant is an agreement which should be executed by two parties. When man needs an agreement with God, the word of approval of God is necessary and it must come from Him. The question is—"How to know that God approves?" The story goes that in this difficult question the brain of a Khasi met its most "head-boiling challenge". They say that the Khasi's attempts and experiments to find an answer were numerous and they took a long time.

The parable of *Ka Krem Lamet Ka Krem Latang* tells us that the sun was fetched from *Krem Lamet Krem Latang*. To those unfamiliar with the parable it seems as if that *Krem Lamet Krem Latang* is situated somewhere beyond the hills. After a good deal of tests it was found that the cock was the suitable representative of man to stand before God. Accordingly after the performance of certain rituals the cock is brought to stand before the altar and tne ceremony follows where signs and marks are asked for from God. This having been done, a word of satisfaction from God comes forth and this expresses the approval of God. And with this the agreement which is the covenant between man and God becomes effective. It is on the basis of "reason" and "covenant" that a Khasi upholds and establishes his religion. The covenant turns to be the commandment or law to mankind and as long as man cherishes the covenant and abides by the commandment or law to go in the way of righteousness, live in righteousness, do everything that is righteous and earn for righteousness; as long as his life here in the world exists, there is no other power on earth to topple him down.

When a Khasi suffers affliction or there is any abnormal condition in his family or private life, he believes that there is a cause behind it and he remembers the covenant. He believes that there must have been some breach of the commandment of God and that he has been given away to the other powers to be punished. In order to find out the cause he makes divine consultation through *Ka Shanam* or cowries, egg-breaking or ritual of cock. He has to do this in order to know his account with God and find out his mistakes of omission and commission. For this reason the Khasi religion is sometimes referred to as *Ka Niam Shat Ka Niam Khein*. This is all but an empty remark without any reason or truth in it.

*Ka Shat ka Khein* which belongs to the ceremonial aspect of the religion is not the religion itself but only a means which a Khasi employs to find out the causes of the displeasure of God.

When a man has found out the causes of the displeasure of God and also the evil spirit to which God has given him away for punishment, he performs a ceremony of sacrifice (called *Ka loit ka law*) to gain atonement for his lapse(s) followed with a prayer of thanksgiving to God. This practice has unfortunately given rise to the idea that the Khasi religion is a "devil worshipping religion" (*Ka Niam Mane Ksuid.*) This is a himalayan blunder. At no time is a Khasi a devil worshipper. He is of course scared of the devils and he happens to be so because the religion teaches him so. There is no other creature who is more horrible to a Khasi than a *Nongaiksuid* (a person who sells himself away to the devil and in connivance with the latter, spends his time and efforts to find fault with his fellow human beings and deliver them to his master the devil by acts of sorcery, etc).

The Khasi's religion is an integral part of their clan and group life. The clan keeps religion in the care of the Godhead, the Ancestress, the Ancestor and the Ancestral Uncle. These four comprise the family cause (*ka Daw iing*). The Godhead here is the God of the clan (*'Leilongkur 'Leilongjait)* which is one of the names a Khasi gives to God. This Godhead is the Supreme Commander and Ruler (*Ka Nonghukum bad Ka Nongsynshar*) who takes care and looks after the clan as a whole. The Ancestress (*Ka Iawbei*) is the great grandmother or the first known mother of the clan, who founded the clan and because of whom the succeeding generations flourish. The succeeding grandmothers are simply called Junior or Modern Ancestresses (*Ki Iawbei Khynraw*) as it is they who continue to swarm the pedigree. The Ancestor (*U Thawlang*) is the great-grandfather or the first known father, husband of the great-grandmother. The Ancestral Uncle (*U Suidnia*) is the great grand-uncle (maternal) who has founded the religion and rites in his own clan and who has collected all the bones of the dead brothers and sisters and nephews and nieces of the clan and interred them in one clan cairn.

When the Godhead (*Ka Blei*), the Ancestress (*Ka Iawbei*), the Ancestor *(U Thawlang)* and the Ancestral Uncle *(U Suidnia)* are all satisfied with the clan or family, no devil or evil spirit or any other cause like the *Dawlum Dawwah* (external cause) can shake or put the clan into trouble. When there is any unpleasant event or happening a Khasi believes that there must be something in the *Dawiing* and when he finds out there is some uneasiness or displeasure on the part of the Godhead he prays for atonement and makes up for his lapses before the composite *Dawiing*. He trusts the *Dawiing* and stands steadfast by it and when he realises that he is without blemish before the *Dawiing* he never allows his heart to be troubled.

A Khasi has no church, house or temple to worship God whereas each and every clan or group has its own *iingseng iingkhatduh* (the residence of the youngest in the lineage of each clan) where all necessary religious rites and ceremonies of the religion are performed. It is in this *iingseng iingkhatduh* where all brothers and sisters belonging to the family or the clan assemble together. It is the duty also of this *iingseng iingkhatduh* to collect the income from the ancestral properties as well as *U synniang u bynhei* (a cash subscription from each adult member of the clan, group or family) to complete and perform all the religious rites pertaining to the family or the group which includes all the married members, male and female. This *iingseng iingkhatduh* must also observe and perform the ritual ceremony of *Ka Phur Ka Siang*—a ceremony by which the bones of the dead members of the clan or family or group of the same ancestress, which lie in separate temporary places by the burning site after the funeral, are collected from different places or villages to be interred in the clan's stone cairn called *Mawbah* where all the bones of the long bygone dead were collected together from time to time. This ceremony is held after due approval is obtained from God in divine consultation. The uncle (maternal) in the family is the priest who is to perform all the religious rites which are to be done in the *iingseng iingkhatduh*.

When any family falls into affliction or distress or financial deterioration or is inflicted with sickness or events causing grief or agony to the family, the family believes that there is a cause behind such happenings. A Khasi does not believe that things take place without a cause and when such things happen he believes that something has offended and displeased the composite *Ka Dawiing Ka Dawsem*. The family resorts to divine consultation to find out the cause. They ask for the clue or sign from grains of rice, or cowries or other materials and should those not yield any result they use the egg-breaking or cock sacrificing ritual. When they have discovered the cause, they, then, perform sacrifices for atonement of the shortcomings so that they may be set free from the gripping affliction, etc., also promising to offer thanksgiving to God who is "the Supreme Commander and Ruler". In case they do not get at the cause in spite of trying all the prescribed ways and means, then the family takes the last resort which is to submit itself humbly before God with prayers for mercy and sympathy. In the prayer they conclude their submission saying, "As ye Godhead will have it". If any eventuality takes place after this exclusive surrender the family grieves no longer and reconcile themselves to their lot as being an ordinance and the will of God.

In general Khasi religious rituals take place within a family household, or in a clan or in a group with its own ancestress, ancestor and ancestral uncle. All religious rites, be it *Ka tap kpoh* (sacrifice to invoke the blessings of God to an expectant mother for her good health and safe delivery), or *Ka Ksan Rngiew* or *Ka jer khun* (ceremony of choosing and giving a child its name), or *Ka iap briew* (performing the rituals at the time of death till the dead body is committed to the funeral pyre), or *Ka Thepmawbah* are all under the purview of *Ka Blei* and *Ka Iawbei* (the Godhead and the Ancestress). If the *Dawlum Dawwah* comes to molest somebody it is only because the *Dawiing* is not at peace and is disturbed and to pacify and satisfy that, they are to pay homage and submit their prayers to the *Dawiing*. This is quite clear in the prayer said after a man has recovered from sickness or from any other kind of afflictions. One of the modes of submission and thanksgiving is as follows :

> Do please hear oh God, oh Ancestress, since now I have found the cause and your reason to have felt offended and transgressed against; now, oh Lord of thousand mercies, do take pity on me: Now as I have fallen into ignorance, I have turned my ways behind Thee, I, a poor human, do give me sound health, for which reason I shall now hence stand awake. . . .

# 4

## *The Devils*

THERE are, according to the Khasi, different kinds of "devils" or evil spirits. Ghosts, for instance, form one such class. The Khasi believe that the body of a man after death returns to the earth but the soul proceeds to the Mansion of God to be with his relatives in the midst of his ancestress and ancestral uncle just as they were together here on earth. But there are individuals who have committed unpardonable sins and are condemned; their clanmen have refused to perform the death rituals for them as per the *Niam* and religious rite. The ghosts of such individuals take the form of devils and they turn out to be very ferocious and horrible devils. Their activity consists simply in tempting and tormenting living persons especially their own clanmen and particularly those whose life is on the brink of death. These spirits are here in this nature around us and some of them operate in groups while others do it singly.

There is another group of devil ghosts who are of good nature. These comprise spirits bearing the lingering souls of those individuals whose *Niam-iap* (death rites) could not be performed for reasons beyond the control of their clanmen, and whose bones could not be taken to the clan's stone cairn by their living fellow-clansmen. These spirits also hover in nature and some of them dwell in a group but most of them like to operate singly. These spirits are not the subjects of *Ka Tyrut*, the queen of evil spirits. These spirits are wont to avoid human beings and when they happen to come across men, it is by a mere freak or chance. A Khasi believes that these spirits live in terrible anguish at their own sad lot that they have been shorn of their religious privileges and go unaccounted for, for no fault of theirs.

Other kinds of evil spirits are *Ksuid-lum* (hill or wood devils), *Ksuid-wah* (water devils) and *Ksuid-suin* (air devils). These make their dwellings respectively in the hills or woods or trees or caves, in the streams or rivers or in the atmosphere. These devils are malicious and never cease to exercise their devilish power over any one when they get the opportunity. A person caught by them is said to be under the trap of *ki lyngkhuh ki pakhuh*. Some of these devils a Khasi calls *ki ksuid mynsaw* as those devils are the souls of some persons who died of accidents, or were killed for their criminal behaviour in the woods or jungles. These devils cause all sorts of disturbances and troubles to the minds of the living beings who chance to go to places where they frequent. When caught by them and duly confirmed so by divine consultation, a Khasi ideally claims his superiority over all such creatures, by calling the devils concerned to his presence and claiming his right not to be disturbed by them on the surface of this earth. He offers betel nuts or a plate of rice or a warm place by the hearth to them but sooner or later he orders the devils to leave the house for their own abode in peace.

Some of these "devils" are called "gods" by the Khasi and are given such offerings as they may demand. Some people offer them a fowl or a pig and sometimes even a goat. These actions are a result of fear psychosis. Amongst the noted ones are *u Rih* which gained much imminence in the regions of Ri Bhoi and Ri Rmen (in north-east Khasi Hills) and in Ri war Ri Thor (in south-west Khasi Hills and south-west Jaintia Hills). *U Rih* is a "hill devil" and sometimes it is called a "malaria or fever devil" owing to the fact that people encroaching the area supposed to be its abode are usually inflicted with fever and malaria. Then there is *ka Niangriang* or *ka Kyian* water beetle which is a water "devil". This causes watery fluid or pus to deafen the ears of children using or playing in the water which is supposedly habited by them. Then there is a water devil known as *ka Lei Kupli* which troubles some people who cross the Kupli river. There are also "air devils" like *U Trang* and *U Rwaibah* which cause heartache to human beings. There are also other "devils" bearing names such as:

*U Blei Synteng, U Kyrtep, U Moisong, U Tynjang, Ka Thapbalong, Ki Puri, Ki Diaw, Ki Boit* and others.

At times of spiritual decay when a Khasi loses his confidence in God, he may take resort to worshipping and offering thanksgiving and sacrifices to the devils. He gives in to all the demands of the devils. However, there have always been others who uphold their origin and their relationship to God and to their fellowmen, they still know the power of God and of His judgment, they understand the true significance of valuing righteousness and justice and also are aware of the assembly of the devils (Pandemonium) seeking power to control over man. Such members of the Khasi society do not care for or fear those who have worshipped and paid tribute to the devils. They count them merely as a disruptive and disturbing influence on mankind. Such a man walking on the hill side or walking through a deep jungle or climbing the high peaks or crossing a stream or a river fears no devil as he has his own powerful reason with which to combat these devils and they shun his proximity. When they would follow him to his home he gives them a betel nut or a plate of rice and bids them to return to their abode. An uncle of the family, who still has not lost faith in God, can, merely by smelling the body of his relative returning from the jungles with high fever, at once sense that *U Lyngkhuh U Pakhuh* has followed the man and would send someone to escort this evil spirit to its own abode via the tri-junction nearest to the village.

In contemporary Khasi society, there are people who have no fear of sins of incest and sacrilege and keep the devils as their household deities and worship them. These deities bring the keepers wealth material prosperity and splendour. These deities are of different types having different qualities. Amongst these the less evil are *Ka Lei Khuri, Ka Raliang, Ka Taro, Ka Lasam, Ka Sabuit* and others and the ferocious ones are *Ka Shwar, Ka Bih* and *U Thlen*. Families who keep these devils as their household deities *(U Phan U Kyrpad)* have their own way of worshipping these deities and offering sacrifices to keep them content, failing which the deities will bring ruin and even death to the members of the family or the household which keeps them.

*Ka Lei Khuri* is a she-devil which renders protection to the family, which keeps her from thieves and helps bring prosperity to it. This deity dwells in the *three stones constituting a hearth (Mawbyrsiew)* and causes intestinal trouble to those who pick up a quarrel or make enmity with its keepers.

*Ka Raliang* is another household deity usually kept mostly by the people who stay in the area of Mawshai—east of Rapleng Peak (in Khyrim Syiemship). Its influence spreads over people whom its keepers love or like. When the keeper says to someone "Oh dear, your calf is so nice" that person's calf will somehow suffer from some pain or it will swell with cankerous trouble or some such-like diseases. For cure the affected must go to the keeper(s) who alone can remove the ill effect caused by their household deity. There is also a belief that if one person is affected in this way by *Ka Raliang* for three times, such a person will automatically acquire the powers of the keeper of this deity and affect someone likewise.

*Ka Taro* brings suffering to those who borrow money from its keeper or to those who might squander the keeper's earnings. This deity would sometimes even visit the close friends of its keeper. The sufferings brought by it are of diverse nature. For cure of the affliction caused by this deity the victim must repay the debt owed to its keepers, or return the benefit derived from using the keeper's earnings. In the case of the keeper's friends suffering from *Ka Taro's* visit the affected persons' family must visit the house and pick up a quarrel with its keepers, and, as a result of the quarrel the friendship must cease to be.

It is difficult to oppose *Ka Taro* for the reason that if the borrower takes a loan from its keeper, the amount of the loan is supposed to belong to this household deity and not to its keeper. If the borrower has cash in hand the entire amount borrowed should be paid back, if no ready cash is available the borrower has to submit himself to *Ka Taro* in prayer with a promise that the loan taken will be paid and as a token of this promise he must throw out from his house a coin or two after the prayer.

In all cases where a victim prays for the removal of the evil influence of these deities, he must, in his prayers, emphasize the fact that in exercising such influence the deities have transgressed the bounds of righteous behaviour.

Then comes *Ka Phan Sabuit* (*sabuit*=deity). This deity causes stomachache and intestinal pain. A Khasi rubs common lime on the fruits grown in the open before taking them—such as bananas, pineapples and the like—in order to get rid of the effects of this *Ka Sabuit*. Even to this day, for instance, it is fairly common practice to put a little lime on a pineapple before eating it. This is to ward off possible evil effects of *Ka Sabuit* or *Dud-Sabuit* beforehand. A Khasi believes that if we take a pineapple without counteracting the *Sabuit* we will most likely suffer from stomachache. While rubbing lime on the pineapple one is also supposed to say the following words:

> Flee away thou *Ka Sabuit ka Sakai*, go to thine own habitation; God has not ordained thee to exercise thy power over mankind.

There are many ways to counteract the power of *Ka Sabuit* and these differ from place to place. But the most common is the one where betel leaf or a palm leaf is used. The leaf is scorched in a fire, and the following arguments is offered in prayers and submission:

> Curse thee, *Ka Sabuit* thou shouldst quietly and peacefully go back to thine own habitation—go to thine owners and keepers who keep thee and worship thee. Wherefore comes thou hither? Should there be any mistake, any shortcoming, it is for us human beings to make amends. . .

After this lime is rubbed on the stomach of the victim and the following words are uttered:

> We who knoweth thee not will bury you under the burning ashes.

Then the leaf is thrown into the burning fire or buried under the ashes with the following concluding exhortation: "Thou should depart at once, God, the Lord has not ordained thee to cast thy power over mankind".

Some of the more ferocious of the devils kept and worshipped as household deities are *Ka Shwar* and *Ka Bih*. *Ka Shwar* torments its victim by strangling him or twisting his neck and two rounds of its twisting proves fatal to the victim. The victim of *Ka Shwar* is a horrible and awful sight and those who are acquainted with the devil's power do not wonder at it. It works against those who make trouble for or pick a quarrel with its keepers. Only persons who are well versed in the ways of this deity can cast off its evil spell and drive or send it away.

*Ka Bih* (poison deity) is the most widely talked about devil in the land of the Khasi. It is of various types and works in different ways and degrees according to the *Jingiatang* (mutual agreement between two parties—here between the deity and the keeper—involving strict and serious conditions binding each side) with those who keep it. There are types of poison which work very slowly and entail chronic pain and slow death, while some others act so fast that death takes place almost immediately. These poisons are also associated with the 'deity of riches'. To counter the power of the poisons is very difficult; the best efforts of specialists in the field of medical herbs frequently fail.

The most ferocious among all the household deities is *U Thlen*. *U Thlen* is terror itself, and frequently the idea of this devil has been the basis for ridiculing the Khasi people. This devil demands human blood from its keepers and they are to pacify and satisfy it and should they fail, it would set its power against them by first putting them to shame before the world and thence by devouring or causing death to the keepers themselves. This devil can take any shape or form though the common belief is that it takes the form of a snake. When those who keep it and give offerings to it cannot satisfy this devil, it takes the shape of a fish or a cat and gets to the roof top to bring shame to the keepers before everybody.

Those who keep this devil are to offer it only human blood and for this reason, they become *U nongshohnoh briew*. One of the methods adopted by the keepers to get a human being into their grasp is to cut off a little of his hair or a bit of his garment and then to offer this in some kind of a sacrifice by means of which the *rngiew* of the victim is captured to give as an offering to *U Thlen*. Another way is to chase and capture the human being physically and kill him. If there are not sufficient males in the family to hunt for human beings they engage mercenary hands to procure victims and "to encourage" such hands they drug them with *ka 'Iad tangsnem* (the liquor which was preserved for a year and consecrated to the deity itself). Having taken *ka 'iad tangsnem* they become more or less insane and turn wild and spirited in their job. After they have killed someone they would take a little amount of blood in a small container to the owners who will then offer it to *U Thlen*. Once the deity has been appeased and satisfied, the household of the keepers flourishes and wears a look of splendour.

It is a Khasi belief that when a man's *rngiew* is firm, neither *U Thlen* nor the *Nongshohnoh* can gain control over him. Even the decorating loose fibres at the hem of the *jainsem* (embroidered upper apron or garment loosely worn across the shoulders by Khasi women) of a woman whose *ka rngiew* is still firm appear to the eyes of a drugged murderer (*nongshohnoh*) as big as whipping ropes and this is sufficient enough to frighten him. Frequently, in order to capture the *rngiew* of the victim, a *nongshohnoh* throws *U Khaw Tyndep* or *U Khaw rawai* (rice grains of yellowish colour offered and sacrificed before *U Thlen* which, thus, has the power to enchant and bring temporary numbness or senselessness to a person on whom it is thrown). Before throwing the rice the *nongshohnoh* justifies himself by saying this :

> Lo! I myself have not done anything to anybody by force, nor have I dragged anyone by might as done by the crows and the kites. With all my rituals have I called you and how can I help when you are destined to die.

They might waylay a victim by hiding in his path. While preparing to throw the rice at him the *nongshohnoh* might also say:

> Behold! what else can I say when you yourself are treading upon this path by your own will. Do not say that by force of might have I done this.

After he has said this he looks at the grains of rice and tosses them in his hand, then he throws the rice at his would-be victim and concludes :

Now, you catch hold, tie up and bind by yourself.

People on whom *U Khawtyndep* is thrown feel almost insane, become numb and paralysed. They can however help themselves if they have the presence of mind by taking a bit of soil from mother earth and thrusting it in their mouth. As soon as this is done the evil spell of *U Khawtyndep* will vanish. If this does not come to the mind of the victim and if no one happens to pass by him, the murderers will have him at their mercy. If one finds such victims of *U Khawtyndep*, they are to be taken away at once from the spot where they are found and brought home. On reaching home it is advisable to perform the ceremony of *Ksan rngiew*.

A Khasi believes that rice which supports human life is also a source of the power with which to protect man from the clutches of the devil. This is the reason why a Khasi never sets out from his home on a journey without taking some grains of rice in his pocket. He can throw this rice back at a *nongshohnoh*, if such a one attacks him with *U Khawtyndep*. In a way it can be said that this is some sort of *U Khawtyndep* to use in return of the *nongshohnoh*. In the event of a *nongshohnoh* approaching him, he takes out this rice and says the following :

> Behold oh Ye Lord from on high, look Ye on me a human being. I am treading on my own way and I never have any mind to take away anybody's life. I am struggling to earn my daily bread as Thou Oh God has disposed.

He moves the rice in his hand and proceeds :

> Those who aim to destroy and do away with life, cut them to death, oh ye, rice. Once they forget the way as planned by God let them forget the shining of the sun and the lighting of the moon. Once they have transgressed the law of God let them be away from the sun, let them be away from the moon.

The *nongshohnoh* will just stand where he is and will be struck numb as if with drowsiness. He will be devoid of any sense or power of action. Some may like to only deal a kick or two or give as many blows as they like with the finger knuckles on their heads and others may even take their lives; but those who can distinguish between the right and the wrong and have professed to do what is right will not choose to do any such thing. A Khasi believes that when all is right with *Ka Dawiing* and when *Ka Rngiew* is firm and unwavering no devil can gain control over him. A Khasi who believes in God and puts his trust in Him is never afraid of any devil or *U Thlen.* The strength of God accompanies him and he *knows* how to protect himself.

A Khasi believes that the devils, fairies, hill-devils, water-devils and others are all but a mess of countless evil-doers waiting only to bring suffering and trouble to mankind. When *Ka Dawiing* is not well these creatures can seize men in the woods or streams or on lonely paths. When caught in such a way a Khasi makes sure of the cause and proceeds with his rituals to get rid of them and offers his thanksgiving to God. A Khasi is afraid of *Ka Tyrut* which is the queen of all devils. This is the greatest foe to a Khasi family. A Khasi believes that unnatural deaths taking place in the open, or from accidents or a mother suffering during her pregnancy are all on account of *Ka Tyrut*. When such deaths take place a Khasi has to find out the cause through usual divination and rituals and has to perform the ceremony of *Mait Tyrut* to cleanse the family of any taint (*raibi*). The dead bodies of those dying an unnatural death or dying in the open are not brought into the house because of the fear that *Ka Tyrut* might enter the family. A Khasi does not allow a conceiving woman either to go to a house where there is a dead body or to attend a funeral because *Ka Tyrut* may take into captivity the poor child in the womb.

THE KHASI MILIEU

## Marriage

**Plate 1:** Riopassah, the groom on reaching the bride's house

*Facing page 48*

**Plate 2:** The groom (4th from left) with friends and relatives listening to the invocation to Ublei

*Facing page 49*

# 5

# *Life*

A GOOD man bases his life in this world on reason and God's commandment and thesc hold fast and support him throughout his life as well as his close kith and kin. He does not believe that his coming to this world is a vain thing or is accidental and without any purpose. He believes that God has created mankind with a reason and has planned the course for mankind to follow. Man is the most important of God's creations; it is man's duty, therefore, to take proper care of his life as long as he lives in this world.

The words *Leh than ialade* (excess behaviour against one's own self) are used to refer to the conduct of persons who hate their own selves. No one at home or outside likes a person who indulges in "excessive behaviour against himself". At best people might pity such a person, and his family will be full of sadness and regret. When such a man dies the society does not grieve over his loss. A person who commits suicide also brings curse, not only to his own life but to his family as well. His whole family will be filled with shame and remorse. This kind of death is considered to have been caused by *Ka Tyrut ka Smer* which is to be cleaned and cast away lest it come to stay in the house or family and befool any member of the family into acting treacherously against his own clanmen.

Since a man has come into this world by reason, he must also live by reason. God who created and planned for his life as a human being has given him a place in the entire universe, where there is room for his moral and intellectual growth as well as for luck and good fortune. The supreme strength of man lies in his power to reason. There is no other strength in this world comparable to the strength of reason.

When man uses God's gifts in the right way all is well with him. Man alone is responsible for any inadequacy in his life. In the covenant man concluded with God, his assigned duty is to uphold the status God gave, by submitting himself before God as his Creator and by living righteously, behaving righteously, working and earning for righteousness and also respecting his fellow men and devoting himself entirely to God. This is but the commandment and when he can truly obey the commandment he will stand unblemished before the Judgment of God and before reason. To live by the commandment and by reason is also to understand the real meaning of dignity.

Reason and commandment to a Khasi, are the obverse and reverse of the same coin of life. To live by the commandment is to live by reason and also the other way round. This world around him is full of difficulties, hindrances and dangers. Besides, the forces of the devils and demons are constantly looking for an opportunity to ensnare and capture man; but when his reason stands firm nothing whatsoever can shake or move him. When a man lives a life of reason his *Ka rngiew* is prominent and his personality shines forth. Blessings of all kinds will flow to him in every effort he is engaged in and goodness will follow him all the days of his life. About such a life a Khasi says: "Reason is at its zenith" (*ka ieng rasong ka daw*). The Khasi word for blessing to anyone who is going to take part in an important competition or to do an important job is therefore—"Hold fast to your own reason". On visiting any patient it is profanity to say, "Fare you well, I'm on my way" on parting, as this means the last greeting on earth. The correct words of greetings instead are: "We are leaving, may luck and reason stand firm with you."

Originally phrases in common use, such as *Ka daw jop* (a cause to succeed) or *Ka daw rem* (cause to lose or fail) were understood in relation to the ideas of reason and commandment. When a man lives by the commandment, his reason is destined to be successful, but when he fails to live by the commandment, his reason is destined to be distorted. Any attempt to achieve success in anything will be in vain. Some obstruction of one sort or another will stand in his way. Sickness and ailments may take place as well as financial crises. His life will be a bunch of riddles. Life too will be a regretful misery and to God he will be a grievous disappointment.

To a Khasi his personal life then is enmeshed in *Ka Dawiing* and it turns to be so since he is a member of the family as well as the clan. He lives in this world not all by himself because he has got the Godhead (*Ka Blei*), the Ancestress (*Ka Iawbei*), the Ancestor (*U Thawlang*) and the Uncle (*U Suidnia*) composing the *Dawiing*. The cause of his family or his clan may turn to be his personal cause and vice-versa. To separate these two is impossible. The idea which dominates here and which is also an important idea in Khasi religion is that a man has a personal and immediate responsibility not only to himself but to his clan or group. He is therefore duty-bound before he sets out to do anything, to envisage the implications of his action himself so that what he proposes to do will be reasonable before God, and his fellow men. A man who cannot understand this is regarded as family-less or clan-less.

It is the duty of every Khasi to think of the consequence of his action before he undertakes it. This process of thought is called *Ka Khan*. It means "to base on reason" any contemplated action before doing it. It should be considered reasonable before God and before his fellow men as indicated before. In marriage, for instance, any uncertainty concerning this generates the fear that the *raibi* or *taint* of this failure may come to his own family or clanmen. In important functions or deeds he proposes to do, in particular, he should consult God through divination, for he is afraid that what he does may turn back against himself and become *Ka Daw Rem* (cause destined to lose). A Khasi believes that of all creatures it is only man whom God wants to know himself first before he jumps at any conclusion regarding others (*tba ia la ka lyngthohdoh*). *U Suid-tynjang* (a lame devil residing in the forests) or any other devil has not this capacity and therefore man, before his doing anything is to first determine and examine his own self before he comments on others as well as before he sets out to do anything.

Science says that when there is a cause there must be an effect, or vice-versa. Though life is full of manifold mysteries—a Khasi believes that not a single event takes place without any cause. When a man sustains injury, while working on his land or walking through a jungle, no treatment is given to his injury until after a "divine consultation" to find out the cause, as it is believed that no such accident could take place without any cause thereof. When there is any strange event taking place in the personal life of an individual or in the family, a Khasi believes that there must be a cause which might relate to personal or to *Ka Dawiing*. He takes it that somehow he has incurred the displeasure of the Godhead or that the Ancestress, or the Ancestor and the Maternal Uncle have been aggrieved and dissatisfied. In such an event he has to try to find out the cause. He uses grains of rice or *Ka Shanam* or *Ka Kub* (large pods containing the seeds of a creeper) or cowries or breaks an egg or takes to ritual sacrificing a cock to find out the cause, and after he has found out the cause he performs rituals to set himself free from the effects or the events, and thence he submits in supplication to the Godhead and the Ancestress in whatever way required of him.

A Khasi believes that he alone is responsible for his own life. For any circumstance or event in his personal life or in that of his family or his clan, he believes that there is a cause behind it which has to do with himself and he never attributes nor shifts the cause to God, or to any other agency. He neither blames his own destiny nor the stars—as some attribute their ill-luck to the stars—but he believes the cause to be his own doing that somehow he has failed to keep the covenant and has turned his back to the commandment. A Khasi's usual response to a misfortune is *Nga uba la ia pan hi la ka hukum* (I myself asked for it).

A Khasi believes that he comes into this world through God's commandment and will be here for a brief sojourn. He must therefore live in perfect harmony with his fellow men as well as in unison with God. This life is his life and he is to be responsible for himself. When he turns his back on the commandment he violates the covenant and in this situation he is a condemned being; as such he is to wake up and force himself to start his life anew—this time in tune with the commandment. As man is the source of all causes of misfortune it is man who is to take the lead to regain the status of a full-fledged and untainted man who keeps the commandment. God is only there to safeguard and ensure the fulfilment of the covenant (*ba ap jutang U Blei*)*. Sometimes man betrays religion and gives a fellow-man or a devil the place of God thus causing sacrilege (*Ka Siar ka Lait-kylla*)—which results in the failure and decadence of man himself.

But God knows that man as a creature is weak and full of mistakes and shortcomings because of which he (man) always prays to God, as he knows that God is full of mercy. In all his prayers and supplications man calls God by the name, "Supreme Commander" (*Nonghukum*). And when the sacrificer is at his wits' end having failed to find out the cause of his grief and of the displeasure of God, he wails in submission to God in the following way:

> Oh! Lord, Supreme Commander, Ye Designer and Dispenser of Life, I can no longer trace my first Mother Ancestress, my first Father Ancestor, I am left in the dark, bewilderment has taken over me; I depend only on Your kind sympathy upon me, Oh Ye God on the surface of this earth and on high.

*Taken from *Ki Dienjat U Longshua* chapter on *Shaphang U Blei*.

# 6

# *Family Structure*

KHASI believe that the family is the foundation of the clan and of the entire race. Therefore, when a Khasi sets up home or begins family life he has to ponder and judge properly so as not to act wrongly. A family usually consists of a mother and a father and the children sitting around the hearth under a roof. Should it be the family of the youngest mother (*iing khadduh*) it also includes the bachelor maternal uncles and also, most likely, the orphaned nephews and nieces who are looked after often by the youngest heir. The family may also include the surviving grand-parents.

The foundation of the family, on the other hand, is not the parents but children. A couple without issue cannot, under any circumstances, build a family. If they continue to live without children they are likened to poor orphans who will only evoke the sympathy of the fellow villagers and the relatives of both clans. There is no objection should they get divorced and frequently there is pressure for a divorce from the relatives of both the husband and the wife if the marriage is considered not to have been proper.

Though the mother, the father and may be others also are by the hearth side, the fire burns more brilliantly under the roof where there are children. The wife becomes a mother and the husband a father because of their children. It is they who form the bond of parenthood and the link of cordial relationship between the two clans of the mother and that of the father. To the mother the children are united in flesh and blood and to the father by his seed of generation. To their clansmen they are "diamonds and rubies" and to the father's clansmen they are "blossoms and fruits".

Right from their childhood the parents' attempt is to bring up their children in a way so that they may learn to live in perfect harmony with their fellowmen as well as in unison with God. They are taught to love and respect their own clan relatives as members of a longer family who are given names with proper identification marks like *Meisan* (eldest mother—eldest sister of the mother), a *Meiŋah* (younger mother—younger sister to the 'elder mother' or to the mother), a *Meideng* (middle mother—a middle sister of mother), a *Meirit* (Young mother—younger sister of mother) and a *Meiduh* (Youngest mother—youngest sister of mother). They are also taught to address a grandmother as *Mei-Ieij* (darling mother) and *Pa-Ieij* (darling father) to grandfather. The maternal uncles are addressed as *Mabah* (eldest uncle), *Maheh* (second eldest uncle), *Madeng* (middle uncle), *Marit* (younger uncle) and *Maduh* (youngest uncle). These uncles have a warm and loving relationship with their nephews and nieces.

Among the father's clan relatives, the *Meikha* (father's mother) is like a goddess to his children. Then come one by one—the *Kharangbah* (eldest aunt), *Khadeng* (middle aunt), *Kharit* (younger aunt) and *Khaduh* (youngest aunt). The children are taught to give to these aunts of theirs all their love and respect, when the aunt visits them, their home seems flooded with joy and wealth in spite of material poverty. But there is also a tremendous sense of awe which the paternal aunts inspire in children. Their emotional status within the larger family circle is so high that children must face them with submission and humility.

When children are sick a visit from the paternal grandmother is like a visit from the goddess. A child is especially moved when the paternal grandmother would take his hand with her blessings and benedictory prayer; this fills his mind with a sense of security and contentment. When the grandmother moves her lips to say, "Oh child ! Why should you ail at all ? I, your (paternal) grandma, wish you all luck and good health that henceforth you rise and run up the hills and down the glades, that you go to the market place, that you move about with your daily work and you attend to your means of earning your bread and butter", the patient feels as if his suffering and ailment have just vanished into thin air.

The relationship between children and their parents is very different from all other relationships with fellowmen. It is too profound for ordinary human mind to fathom and therefore it defies description. For an aunt to get offended is not a pleasant thing; but for a father to wail and cry out of disappointment is a grave matter indeed; and the family will sooner or later meet with a sad eventuality. For the children to say "*They* are only the source of our birth" is a gigantic profanity to a Khasi. When the children go on a visit to their paternal grandmother or aunts they take with them *numerous gifts* to them and when asked "Why at all do you bring so much ?" The right answer is "Oh dear Grandma (or Aunties) : These are not ours—they are yours. If you have not given us, where shall we get anything from ?" When the paternal grandmother dies and it is time that her bones are put in the *Mawbah* (clan's cairn) the grand-children are to perform ritual of *Ka Phur Ka Siang* to prepare themselves to go and attend the ritual of *Ka nguh Meikha Pakha.* They are to take with them a pig for sacrifice and an ox for the *Ka Phur ka Siang.* They bow down three times before the grandmother and then perform three rounds of sword dance (*Shad wait*), with the paternal uncles or their father's clanmen. They dance the first round and they bow down their heads to the uncles and other clanmen who are dancing with them and continue in this fashion till the end of the third round.

In a house, where brothers and sisters live in great emotional closeness to one another with their mother at sight, the love and nearness which reign supreme over them is beyond human description. Flesh of the flesh and blood of the blood is what binds them fast together. Brothers and sisters since their childhood have been taught and trained to love and respect one another to identify themselves as *Bah heh* (eldest brother), *Bah deng* (middle brother), *Bah rit* (younger brother) and *Bah duh* (youngest brother) as well as *Kong heh* (eldest sister), *Kong dong* (middle sister), *Kong rit* (younger sister) and *Kong duh* or *I duh* (youngest sister). They are taught never to find fault with one another as no one is faultless. They are not to be distant or aloof even from one another, because, come what may, it is not proper for any of them to forsake own kith and kin. The eldest son is a "deputy uncle" who helps the eldest uncle of the family and the clan.

A father's status in the family is unique. He is the main pillar supporting and sustaining the family. The sound of his *hookah* brings security to the household and his coughing symbolises the strength and power that controls the whole household. He knows his status and duty as a father and over and above that he does not aspire for more. In his clan's family he is the uncle and in his children's family he is the father. As a father he earns for his children and enhances his earnings for his children's wealth and progress. He bides his tongue but his children are taught to show respect and not to behave in a way which displeases him or causes any dissatisfaction to him. At night, along with the mother, he and the children would sit around the warm hearth and he would impart advice to them and they would exchange views towards greater mutual understanding and well-being of the family.

If a family has the youngest heir of the group or clan, it is the custodian of the clan and the *Iingseng-Iingkhadduh*. The family collects the inherited ancestral wealth and also gathers together in the family all those nephews and nieces, the kith and kin, and those who are orphans and forlorns, and gives them their daily bread and shelter so that they will not become fugitives or wander about and also to save them from starvation and begging, particularly, so that the neighbours will not get a chance to speak ill of the family and thus prevent any shame that may affect the pride and prestige of the clan in general and the family in particular. The youngest mother of this family judges and arbitrates over whom to pull up and whom to give the necessary help. She also strives on to enhance family earnings and thus increase its wealth. Her family's cooking pans are big but then her earnings must watch them. The eldest uncle (maternal) performs all the rituals, pertaining to the family and the clan, in this family's house. These are as *Ka Iingseng Iingkhadduh*. The youngest mother and custodian of the clan gathers and collects all the bones of the dead clanmen which are to be deposited in the cairn. Before the bones are put into the *Mawbah* the custodian of the rites collects *U Synniang U Bynhei* (contributions) from all members of the clan to perform *Ka Phur ka Siang* to enshrine the cause of the religion in each family as well as the clan as a whole, and more especially for those who have already departed from this world to go and join their ancestor (*Iawbei*) and the Maternal Uncle (*U Suidnia*) along with their own kith and kin. This youngest family (*iingkhadduh*) is like a palace full of splendour and prosperity; it is also a warm and comforting place giving shelter to those left orphaned and isolated; and it is also a place of religion which keeps the *U Klong U Ksaw* to fulfil religious obligations and perform all the rites pertaining to the family and to each group and clan. This family is also the custodian and motherly guardian of the rights of the entire clan.

# 7

# Marriage

BROADLY speaking, there are two ways in which marriages are brought about. The first is through engagement arranged by the parents and the relatives of both sides and the second is where the two concerned, the male and the female, choose one another and settle down to set up a family. The second way is what has been adopted by the western people while the first is what is mostly accepted by the eastern people. Which of the two is better, is still a controversy, and from the arguments on both sides it is difficult to arrive at a verdict. As it happens the original Khasi way belongs to the first category—that is, in consonance with the eastern world. Marriage is an extraordinarily serious matter for a Khasi as it is the starting point in the raising of a family, and for that reason to leave this burden only on the children and brothers and nephews is very dangerous. If it is given to their sweet will, it may lead to blunders and future regrets. The parents along with the uncles of the family therefore reserve to themselves this job of giving and taking in marriage of their children.

When there is any male member of the family ready for marriage, the family as a whole consider the matter. Before any selection is made, they first consider and assess the personal qualities of the girl of their choice, and then her family background and other necessary factors. They strive their best to avoid giving a male member of the family to a family having any unpleasant social stigma or whose integrity has been questioned. They particularly avoid those families which are reputed to be keepers of some *household deities*. When they come across any grown up girl of their common consent they send a mediator in the person of an aged and respected man to negotiate and ask for the consent of the girl's family. The girl's family also receives the mediator in a respectful manner and they ask for time before giving any decision or reply, as it is a necessity for them also to sit as a family and consider the matter.

When the girl's family accepts the offer, they keep a date for the "betrothal engagement". On this occasion both the maternal uncles and the father and paternal uncles of either side are to be present along with their friends, relatives and village elders and bear witness to the matter in hand. Prior to the engagement of the two, both families take great pains to uncover inauspicious circumstances, if any, lest any misfortune befall either side which may result in displeasure or dissatisfaction of *Ka Dawiing*. When all signs are clear the betrothal is arranged ceremoniously and the transaction is entrusted to a respected elder who is well conversant with the job. Some do also exchange an engagement or betrothal ring and others perform *ka suit ka shor* ceremony. Once the family elders and members have given their consent to the wedding, seldom would the children or nephews and nieces concerned disapprove or refuse. In the case of poor families, the marriage ceremony is solemnised and celebrated in an austere and simple way—by drinking of rice beer. But when both sides of the families are well off and wish to enjoy the ceremony they make it into a great festive occasion with *pynhiar sati-synjat lat* and *lam ja lam doh* and in normal circumstances nobody in the village goes to work on that day in order to be able to take part in the celebration.

Normally families do not allow their young and minor males to marry as they are afraid that they may misbehave; or the neighbours will speak ill of them or that the family may be looked down upon by the others. A male is to remain until he has served his time at home with his labour to earn his *kamai nongkhynraw* (bachelor's earning). When he is of age for marriage they do not stand in his way nor do they claim his bachelor's earnings. He may give these earnings or property to his clanmen or his brothers, sisters or nephews and nieces or he can take it with him to his wife. There is a practice in many places in the interior of Khasi-Jaintia Hills by which a married man stays in his mother's house after marriage until his wife has borne him an issue or two, and then only he goes to stay permanently with his children. During the time that he stays in his mother's house the married man works and earns for his mother's house and should the children be in any difficulty due to their poverty, he would feed them. During this time he works for and eats in his mother's house and only during the nights he goes to his wife and children.

When the marriage is celebrated by the *Lam ja lam doh* ceremony, a date is fixed commonly acceptable to both the families. Each side arranges or engages a mediator (*U Ksiang*) to add pomp and effect to the ceremony. Throughout the course they try to hold on to the arguments on their own sides and they are ready to come down only when there seems to be a total deadlock in the argument. On the appointed date the bridegroom leaves his house accompanied by his guiding maternal uncles and paternal uncles along with his male relatives and friends after the mother and his maternal aunts have showered him with blessings for his peace and happiness. On the journey he never turns back towards his own house. On the way the party works up a mood of joy and merriment amidst a great deal of applause and laughter. A group of men from the bride's family meets the groom's party half-way and they stop for a while to exchange greetings and betel nuts. Then jointly the group marches in a procession towards the bride's house in the midst of joyous shouting. Just before reaching the house, they dance the *shad lymmuh* (formal group dancing).

On reaching the yard of the bride's house, a serious discussion takes place between the mediators. They proceed to dig out and bring to the surface and hearing of the crowd collected around them, all the arguments to justify the marriage so that all possible mistakes can be avoided and that there will be no regret in the future. After the two sides are satisfied the sacrificer (a diviner who performs the marriage ritual) takes a little liquor from the gourd-flagon brought by the mediator of the male and also from that brought by the mediator of the female. He then mixes the two together in a separate empty gourd-flagon and he performs the ritual of *Ka suit ka shor* to confirm the marriage before the godheads of both the families and invoke their blessings for the event and for their future guidance and help. Before the bridegroom enters the house, the bride's mother anoints the groom's head with oil, welcomes him and gives her blessings to him so that he remains a man of integrity, functions as a full-fledged man and takes the burden of fatherhood of a family. Before the day comes to an end, the members and relatives of the family, the near and distant maternal and paternal relatives, the friends and acquaintances as well as the entire village take the special meal prepared and laid before them. Before their departure to their respective places they see the newly wed couple, bless the two, wish them economic prosperity and loving children. They also advise the new couple to live in continuous love and harmony and never to indulge in squabbles nor quarrels on domestic affairs lest disturbance and offence be caused to *Ka longiing lonesem*.

On the following day the girl guided by her husband along with her maternal aunts visits the house of her husband to pay homage to her mother-in-law. On her arrival, the husband's mother anoints her daughter-in-law's head with oil, blesses her wishing that her family may prosper and multiply abundantly, and achieve goodness and joy. She takes her daughter-in-law to her kitchen-garden or field where the latter would work with a hoe for one or two turns, or pluck out a weed or two in the garden as a token of joint endeavour and co-operation with her mother-in-law at times of hardship and economic crises. At dusk she serves food to her daughter-in-law along with her son, as a token of fact that the mother-in-law's rice pan is also a part of hers. On completion of all the formalities, all return to the girl's house. On the birth of the first child the new parents take the issue to show to the father's mother and the latter takes the new born child in her lap.

The customs and formalities observed differ in detail from one part of the land to another, according to local situation and convenience. The girl's mother keeps the new couple under her care and often advises them and talks to them about the ups and downs of life, about the bad times and the good times so that they will know how to earn and save for their own future security. After the couple are blessed with an issue or two, it is now time for them to start a family home by themselves. The mother-in-law makes ready and gives them utensils for cooking rice and curry, plates to eat from, a circular flat basket (made of bamboo canes used to separate paddy from rice before preparing rice for kitchen purposes) as well as other kitchen accessories to enable her daughter to set up home—another roof to add to the clan's strength and to the joy and magnificence of *Ka lei longkur ka Leilongjait* (the Godhead).

# 8

## *Married Life*

ONE of the foundations of traditional Khasi society is the recognition of the special and unique role of woman in the fabric of society. The thought that after marriage the male and the female become one flesh and one blood is alien to the traditional Khasi view of things. In fact to think of a married woman in this way might even be considered as an act of sacrilege and profanity which might have to be countered by the performance of the ritual *Khasi Tyrut*. The Khasi belief is that a female remains a woman, and must, after marriage, perform the very special role of a mother and enjoy the equally special status that this role carries with it. The husband and wife can never become one flesh and one blood which for a Khasi amounts to belonging to the same clan.

The institution of marriage is neither a covenant nor an agreement or contract, but is a mutual adventure between a woman and a man in a harmonious blend of mind and thought to establish a family. Contracts and covenants are *legal* arrangements, and they cannot be dissolved without going through the due process of law—whatever that process might be; but a Khasi marriage is not thus bound by law. When a husband and a wife find that mutual understanding is no longer possible, and arrive at the conclusion that it will be more painful for them to stay together as husband and wife than if they separate, they take resort to a customary divorce through the simple ritual of throwing cowries or copper coins into the air. After the ritual the separate, and they no longer have any mutual personal obligation to one another, nor any claim on each other. After the divorce ceremony is over, the witnesses present make the following pronouncement :

**Plate 3:** The groom's feet being washed before entering the bride's house

**Plate 4:** Partaking of the ceremonial food and drink

**Plate 5:** Rio, his bride Kamina and her parents

**Plate 6:** (Left to right) the bride's uncle, Kamina, Rio, the bride's father and the groom's father

**Plate 7:** After the ceremony, Rio and Kamina as man and wife

**Plate 8:** (Right to Left) Onderson Mawrie, H. Roy and I.P. Lyndogh

# THE KHASI MILIEU

**Plate 9:** Delegates to a conference on Khasi Religion in the Department of Philosophy, NEHU

**Plate 10:** The Lyngdoh from Sobhar

**U. Klasor Mirchiang performs *Karimphanket* (thanks giving)**

**Plate 11:** The arrow pierces the heart of the pig being sacrificed

**Plate 12:** Rice grains being thrown over the sacrificed animal

> Ho ! Hear, you, people of the village—know ye from now on that *so and so* (a male) and *so and so* (a female) have thrown cowries and made a divorce (*Kynting sbai and lait u san shyieng*) and anyone who wants to have a match with them can do so because now they are both free.

The wife and the husband must, of course, belong to different clans. The female has her own peculiar rites, her own clan's stone cairn and her own Ancestress and Ancestral mother and likewise the male has his own Ancestress and his own clan's stone cairn. Both sides have their own separate *Dawiing-Dawsem*. When the male falls sick it is his clanmen and his own kith and kin who will perform the rituals and sacrifices on his behalf; also the rituals must be performed in his own *Iingseng-Iingkhadduh*. In this matter, his wife cannot impose her will on him. However, if the husband dies, she and her children, will collect his bones and deliver them to his own clan relatives. If the place of the clans of the demised where he actually died are not far apart, the clanmen themselves attend the funeral and collect his bones.

Children are the foundation of family life. A married life without issue is of no value, and without children family life cannot even begin. When a couple remains childless, it should not be surprising if people begin to say such things about them as, "They should not in the first instance, have become man and wife. Their union was destined not to achieve fulfilment" and so on. And should such couples separate in due course, people do not wonder at this, nor are they ever the victims of any social division. For childless couples there are only feelings of sympathy, not only from the members of each family but from the society as a whole. Frequently, relatives of either partner would come up with suggestions of separation. The clanmen of the male might say to him : "Why should you stay there without any child? Come back to your own kith and kin."

Without any child the woman cannot become a mother nor a man a father and as such there can be no family. This only affects not only the couple concerned, but the relatives on either side as well. If a woman is childless, there will be no one to call her sister *Kmienah-kmiesan* (younger and elder sister of mother) and no one will call her brother or "clan brothers", "uncle"; and the man's ties with his family will be also similarly affected. A married life of this sort is like a barren piece of land. Such a marriage is particularly sad for the husband's mother as she will be deprived of the ritual respect and homage paid by grandchildren : it is only her grandchildren who have the privilege to be "recognised" in the course of rituals by the man's mother, so also it is only the man's children who have the privilege to be "recognised" in the course of rituals by his clansmen. His children are looked upon by the man's clan folk as their *blossoms and fruits*. The man's children alone are entitled to the blessings through *grains of rice* ritually thrown at them (*jingshat khaw*) or in sacrifices performed by his clanmen. The mother of the children does not take part in the ritual known as *Ka Nguh Meikha*.

The relation between a father and his children is of a unique nature. They come from his seed and it is for them that he works and labours, he earns and strives to increase his wealth as much as he can. The mother is but a custodian and caretaker of her children. For the father to ill treat his children is a sacrilege. He devotes himself totally to their well-being, and expects, in return, not to be ill-treated by his children or looked down upon by them. If he is poor, he shares his poverty with them and lives from hand to mouth with them; and if he is rich, his wealth is meant only for their well-being. At times of tribulation he suffers his lot with them; and he is happy with them when they are happy. He never expects more than he gives them and he never makes any undue demands on them. It depends on the children to think of his welfare, but for them to ill-treat their own father is profanity itself, and should they so behave their future is bound to be dark. Also society will rise up to judge and condemn openly such an action.

The relation between a husband and a wife rests on the understanding that they have a crucial role to play for the family which they have just started. Their responsibility to their children is profound and over-riding. Neither the husband nor the wife has a position lower than the other in their relationship. A woman has her own status as a mother, and a man his status as a father and it is their business to manage and run their own household according to their wisdom, mutual understanding and cooperation. All mistakes arise from a failure to realise this original norm set by our ancestors in respect of a man and his married life. Ignorance or violation of this norm results in unseemly competition for power and authority between a father and a mother in running the family and as a consequence one side takes to heart the sense of failure and shame which leads ultimately to separation and collapse of the home (*jingpait jingpra u khiewja*). The saying, "A hen has crowed", does not mean that a mother should surrender or submit herself to the father but rather that there is no more goodwill and cooperation and that the mother has overstepped her sphere of activities without taking due cognizance of the father of the family. When a woman no longer understands her status as a mother and the man his status as a father then marriage becomes a total failure.

As both man and woman come from their respective clans, they remain each in their own clan. It is improper and dangerous for a husband to interfere in the community affairs of his wife's clan and equally dangerous for the wife to try and have a say in the clan affairs of her husband. It is difficult for a husband to continue staying with a wife after his clanmen and relatives have completely lost their good faith in her and equally so for a wife to pull on with a man whom her clanmen and relatives now completely dislike. In married life and in the wider relationship with members of the two clans, a couple, therefore, must give way to narrow-mindedness, rigidity of mind or heart, or to personal ambition. All aspects of the married life must be informed by kindness, compromising heart, mutual understanding and above all, love.

A wife must understand that a husband is a person who stands in the middle of two worlds—his first world is his life and responsibility pertaining to his own clan and his kith and kin; and the second is his life and responsibility pertaining to his own children. Any rigid claim on him from either world, places him in a painful position. And this may lead, say, to an unseemly conflict between the father's clanmen and his children, which is often considered the worst thing that can happen to a Khasi. This kind of conflict affects seriously the root or the source of the *longiing longsem* (family life and relationships), the *jinglong kur-jinglong jait* (clan relationship and harmony) and the *longkha longman* (relationships generated through marriage).

In short, a married life for a Khasi means a life of "mutual enhancement for the man and wife". This "mutual enhancement" demands a lot of things. It demands liberal mindedness from both sides and also mutual love and respect. It also demands understanding, generosity, patience, kind-heartedness, mutual trust and joint responsibility. When these govern and guide the married couple the feeling of individual loss on any side disappears and so also any feelings of bitterness, estrangement and the sense of fundamental disagreement. The family which they head achieves a sense of fulfilment while the relationships generated by the marriage will remain pleasant and cordial which will in turn lead to family peace and happiness. "The clanmen will ever remain the clanmen, and the in-laws will ever remain the in-laws".

# 9

# *Lineage*

A GOOD Khasi must conduct his life according to principles laid down in his own tradition and find the right place for everything in accordance with the foundations of Khasi society and in the light of his own native wisdom. A Khasi does not do anything or start anything new without turning to the original principles. He always contemplates on why he has come to the world as a man and how he should uphold his status as a man (*Ka tynrai longbriew manbriew*). Before he sets out to do any thing he consults, by divination, with God. When he takes his clan or lineage from the female he knows very well what he is doing. He is doing this not for his own sake but, in his consideration, to build his whole tribe as one unified and single race. For this reason his adopting the lineage from the female is inter-linked with religion, economy and the administration of the state.

Every Khasi clan or group has its own respective "very" great grand-mother or ancestral mother and from her we descend and multiply. This ancestral mother is the Ancestress. The Khasi believes that God has created not just one ancestress but many and they form the *Hynniew trep Hynniew Skum* (Seven families). When families and groups multiply, the clans constituting the group spread out to different areas of the land. As a queen-bee collects and forges a unified family of all the bees in a hive, so is it with the Ancestress (Iawbei) who collects her children and grand-children and constitutes a clan. All females and successions of females from her womb gradually grow and multiply and these successive "ancestresses" are called *Iawbei-khynraw* (successive or Deputy Ancestresses).

A Khasi believes that when God sees the need he creates still new ancestresses. When circumstances so demand, God devises means for creating a "new ancestress". There are several stories relating to such intervention by God. One of them is *Ka Pahsyntiew.* This woman just came and appeared at *Krem Marai* (Marai cave) which is situated at only about *six arrow-throws* from *Iew-Pursing* (Pyrsing Bazar) at Nongkrem. It is from this woman that emerged the *Jait Syiem Shyllong* (Syiem clans of Shyllong). After she gave birth to two daughters she returned to Marai Cave and just vanished as a fairy. This 'Ka Pahsyntiew' is thus the Ancestress (Iawbei) of the *Syeim clan of Shyllong.* Then there is *Ka Lidohkha* who is the Ancestral-mother or Ancestress of the *Jait Syiem Suinga* and *Syiem Khadsawphra.* This *Ka Lidohkha* came from a fish and she also returned to the pool of the river from which she came, never to show her face again. Whatever one might say about such legends interesting indeed is the remark about *Ka Lidohkha* appearing in *U Nongphira* of 1904 which read, "This does not indicate that a fish has given birth to a human being, it indicates that a woman takes a mysterious form to materialise what God designs".

The clan belongs to no one but the Ancestral mother or the Ancestress and to the successive mothers. They continue the process of generation; the offspring multiply thus consolidating and expanding the clan. There is insecurity in a small or limited clan, and to be part of a large clan is a matter of grace and pride.

There is also a religious reason why a Khasi draws his lineage from the female. In olden times religion used to pervade and regulate every sphere of man's life. It is only during recent times that efforts have proved successful to separate the religion from other spheres of man's life. In olden times to take away the religion of a people was to destroy the life of the people; and this may yet prove to be true for the Khasi. According to the Khasi, the *Ancestress* (*Iawbei*) *is under the Godhead* (*Ka Blei*) *who is God of all clans* (*Ka 'Leilongkur ka 'Leilongjaid*) *who is also the Supreme Commander and Ruler* (*Ka Nonghukum bad Nongsynshar*). It is the Ancestress who looks after all those who spring from her, those dead as well as alive. It is she who is to gather and collect together her offspring whose bones have been interned in the clan cairn (*Mawbah*) and are under the care of the Ancestral uncle (*U Suidnia*) who is the eldest uncle. It is she (the Ancestress) who is to look after those who are alive with, of course, the help of the Godhead (Ka Blei) who is god of the clan (*Ka 'Leilongkur*) and also that of the Ancestor (*U Thawlang*) and the Ancestral Uncle (*U Suidnia*) comprising the "*Dawiing*" (Family Cause). It is for this reason that a Khasi submits in prayer, when he is relieved of pain and suffering, addressing both the Godhead and the Ancestress as follows :

> Do please give ear oh God, oh Ancestress, since now I have found the cause and your reason for feeling offended and transgressed against, now, oh Lord of thousand mercies, do take pity on me. Now as I am aware of my ignorance, I have turned towards you, I, a poor human. Do give me sound health.
> (Rabon Singh's *Kitab Jingphawar-Jingdwai haba la bha*)

In the above thanksgiving prayer after recovery, we see that the Ancestress is complemented by the Godhead. The Ancestress gathers together only those who are her offspring to reinstate in them the religion according to the ordination of God. The ritual of *Ka Tap Lubri* (ceremonial confirmation of a child's name) is chiefly to quell the displeasure or unhappiness of the Godhead, the Ancestress, the Ancestor and the Ancestral Uncle. Sometimes there are cirumstances or events which, through "divine consultation" are found to be as a consequence of sadness or dissatisfaction on the part of the Ancestress, the Ancestor and the Ancestral Uncle as well as those relatives whose bones lay interred in the cairn.

To remove their cause of dissatisfaction submissive prayers and supplications are the better and easier means since those who are to be pacified are of the same family, and often only these prayers and supplications win back their confidence and concurrence.

The Khasi also justify their lineage system in terms of their ancestor's experiences of his daily life. When a Khasi came to the present Khasi Hills he became a busy man. His duty was to keep intact and protect his land, and if possible, to expand his territory. He was a warrior and he gave himself such war-like names as *U Khla ka Wait* (Tiger wielding the sword), *Ki Khun ka Wait ka Stieh* (Sons of the sword and the shield), *Ki Khyndai bah Ryntieh* (Countless number of bowmen) and the like. The blood he has shed for his mastery over these hills is immeasurable and for this reason he has named his land *Ka Ri Umsnam* (the land of bloodshed). A warrior has seldom time to look into family affairs or, for that matter, the lineage, hence it is the duty of the mother to train her children to be part and parcel of her own clan. The Khasi race formerly did not comprise a large population. Hence when a Khasi goes on an expedition of war to the neighbouring plains to expand his territory he captures plainswomen, and brings them into the hills, marries them and gives them names in order to give them and their children the clan. Then he gives them the religion and performs the rites to convert them into Khasis and live as full-fledged Khasis. Clans having the prefix *Khar* are not many and these clans are the groups springing from the ancestral mothers coming from *Ri Dkhar* (the plains). It is these offspring who have expanded the *Hynniew Trep Hynniew Skum* to constitute the Khasi race.

It seems that the founder uncles and fathers who have moulded the Khasi society weighed the right of the mother against the right of the father over their children. And the balance of weight seems to have fallen on the mother's side. It is she who conceives, who counts the period nine months' or ten months' maturation of the infant in her womb, and it is she who bears the labour pain and risks her life at the time of her delivery of the child. It is she who lets the child feed at her own breast, she is the one who keeps awake through the night and her hands wash the child. Children spring from her and they are the flesh of her flesh and the blood of her blood.

The man who paces the length and breadth of this world does not find time to gather and collect together his children. Either he should "knead" the bread (earn bread) or keep the children. To keep and raise the children is not easy, and in any case, it does not fall in line with the male's primary work. This is the work of a woman, and man's work is to devise means and ways for maintenance of the family. He, however, enjoys his dutv as an uncle to keep an eye on the affairs of his clan relatives who are his brothers and sisters, nephews and nieces. He gives to the woman the clan and holds to himself only the string of relation between the two clans which is, symbolically, a "navel" (*U Sohpet u Ksai*).

# 10

## *Children*

SINCE the time a child is inside the mother's womb it has already become a precious soul and a being designed by God. It has already in its own being untold value and dignity. To ill-treat or even speak ill of it is prohibited and a woman who does not have any regard for the child she has conceived is no woman at all. It is improper for a woman even to say, "I have conceived it six months ago". She should instead say "For six months now I have cared for it honourably". Our present generation might feel that at this point we have made a fetish of polite expression; but it simply symbolises the respect and awe with which a Khasi views the very idea of a human life.

Until the child has seen the light of day, the father must be very careful and mindful in his movement and activities as a man. He must not for instance, fire a piece of iron red hot or use it, as a red or purple birth-mark may appear on any part of the body of the child to be born. When he is a regular worker in such a trade or if necessity compels, the would-be father has to plead by saying, "Please move aside my child, father is at work". It is taboo for a father to kill a snake, or to go hunting or use a gun, or to complete the weaving and plaiting of a basket or any bamboo work. For those who do all this out of ignorance, there is still forgiveness, but those who do such things in spite of their knowledge, they can be sure that something will happen to the child in the mother's womb. In the war area (part of the Jaintia Hills district of Meghalaya bordering Bangladesh) a certain man, whose wife happened to be pregnant, joined a hunting group even after all friends cautioned and tried to prevent him. In the jungle he happened to be the first man to shoot a tiger and the animal was hit on the mouth and its upper lip was torn ! His wife was at home at the time. And when their child was born after the incident, a baby girl was born to them but her upper lip was torn. This actually happened at Mawlong (a place 20 Km. from Cherrapunjee, the wettest place in the world, bordering Bangladesh). Another incident took place at Nongsteng in East Khasi Hills District in which a father-to-be saw a snake and killed it even after everyone who knew his wife and were near him told him not to. He hit the snake with a stick on the waist and the snake was killed instantly. When the man's child was born it was found that she had a bone-deformity at the waist and could not even crawl. Many would, of course, laugh at such stories, but life is a mystery, and there is hardly a Khasi who would openly dare violate these prescriptions.

Marriage is an act of purity, and conception in wedlock is similarly pure. Also the child comes into the world in purity. If the labouring mother loses breath while delivering, relatives at hand do ask the father if he had spent nights with women elsewhere during his wife's pregnancy and if so, he should confess it; and similarly the mother should confess if she had betrayed her husband. It is only when both of them have told the truth that the pure child comes peacefully into this world. In case the mother still groans and cannot deliver they take resort to the rituals of egg-breaking and divination and when the counsel comes in the affirmative, either the father or the mother has to confess straightaway, and if still such confession is not forthcoming, the mother's life is endangered, and with this that of the child's. Should the child die, this might even be tantamount to murder.

When a woman is pregnant, a special ritual has to be performed for the expectant mother and the child to be born. This ceremony is known as *Ka tap kpoh* (consecration of the mother's womb). This *Tap kpoh* is a sacrifice and consecration for the mother's physical health and for the safe delivery of the child, offered to the Godhead and the Ancestress. In each and every household there is a gourd specially kept for the ceremony of *Ka tap kpoh* and it is called the *Klong Iawbei* (Ancestress Gourd). This gourd is so preserved in a place that no one will easily gain access to it and it is taken out only when it is needed. Should this gourd crack or break by itself it is believed that this is a bad omen for the father of the child. There are diverse ways in which this ceremony of *Ka tap kpoh* is performed but the common practice is to sacrifice a hen whose legs must be spotless although they may be of any colour. The expectant mother sits on the right side of the person doing the actual sacrifice. She hands over the hen to him to complete the ritual for her. After praising God and reminding himself and other participants of the great design of God in creating man, the sacrificer asks for God's judgment of approval through a sign in the intestines of the hen. If, however, the proper sign is absent, the sacrifice has to be performed again to make good what is wanting.

The ceremony of *Ka tap kpoh* is supposed besides other things, to provide a safeguard against *Ka iap tyrut ka iap smer* which the Khasi are mortally afraid of. A victim of pre-natal death or post-natal death is a case a *Ka iap tyrut ka iap smer*. Such a death is believed to bring greater misfortune to the family than any other kind of death. The *mait tyrut* ceremony has to be performed in order to cleanse the family and the clan of the *Tyrut* and in order that such death does not become habitual. Neither unmarried women nor pregnant women are allowed to attend funerals of victims of such deaths lest *Ka Tyrut Ka Smer* catches hold of them and shows its face in their respective families.

The morning after a child is born the ceremony of *Jer Khun* (naming ceremony) is performed. At this ceremony, the status of the child is asserted by means of obvious symbols. If it is a male child, they keep by the altar a sword, a bow and arrow ; and if it is a girl they keep a *khoh* (conical basket made of bamboo) and *u star* (a head strap generally made of cane). Such is the fear and respect shown to a child that they do not select only one name for him lest the *Dawiing* be displeased or offended. They usually suggest three names and during the ceremony one name is selected out of the three. They consult, through divination, the Godhead and the God of the clan which of the three names they approve. The divination may be by spilling drops of liquor from the gourd or by egg-breaking or by dropping bamboos. If the Godhead along with the Ancestress, the Ancestor, the Ancestral Uncle and also the dead close relatives of the child whose bones had been interred in the cairn, are not happy or satisfied with the name given to the child then that name will not bring good fortune and happiness to the child.

But even all the precautions taken through the naming ceremony are not considered sufficient, there is still the fear that there might be some lingering discontentment on the part of God and the Ancestress. Should it be so, the composite *Dawiing* pertaining to the child will be disturbed and affect the child's future life as a human being. In order to ensure a double protection in this respect for him and the whole family, another ceremony called *Ka Tap Lubri* (confirmation ceremony) is performed. This ceremony is held some time after the child has been given a name. If the child is healthy and is growing well it is believed that all is well and there is no dissatisfaction or displeasure from any quarter. In this ceremony of *Ka Tap Lubri*, a new *jymphong* (hand-woven jacket without sleeves) is presented to a boy and a '*jain kyrshah* or *kansa* (apron) to a girl. It is only after this that the name selected for the child during the preceding name-giving ceremony is confirmed.

On the other hand, should a child, after the name was given, turns to be unhealthy and sickly and not grows as it should, it is believed that there has been discontentment and dissatisfaction on the part of the Godhead, the Ancestress and others whose bones had been laid in the cairn. Under the circumstances, the *Rngiew* and *ka bok ka rwiang* of the child should be set on a firm ground. Another name is chosen to satisfy those concerned. A new garment is given to the child, symbolic of the new life starting under a new name. It is for this reason that sometimes we find some persons with two names. The first name "sticks" in spite of efforts to forget it. If after the ceremony of *Ka Tap Lubri* the child continues to be as unhealthy and sickly as before and there is no sign of improvement in this respect it is inferred that the *dawiing* has ceased to have anything to do in this case. This means that the family, as far as religion is concerned, has become ignorant and is at a loss. They must now surrender the child to the paternal grand-mother for her to do what she can with it. The father's mother takes the child, buys new garments and gives a new name to the child. She gives her blessings to the child saying that she has taken total responsibility for the child, submitting her prayer and supplication to God to give a new life of health, growth and prosperity to the child. This surrendering of a child of one family to the paternal grandmother is known as *Ka Kyrbah Nongkha*. This practice takes place mostly in the Ri War area and it generally occurs in those families and clans who have no more elders and uncles, and as such are no longer acquainted with the religious practices in their families or those who have lost track of their religion.

The Khasi believe that when the child is still in the mother's womb or when it is yet to be an infant in this world, his being is still under the guardianship and protection of the Godhead, the Ancestress. For this reason, the stool passing out of the bowels of a new born who has not been fed with common feed is known as *Ka eit iawbei* (Ancestress stool). When an infants parts the lips smilingly even before it attains self-consciousness, and even sub-consciously laughs by itself, it is said that, it smiles in response to the fondling of the Godhead or the Ancestress (*Rkhie iawbei or Iarain iawbei*). When it moves its lips in a sucking manner it is said that the Godhead and the Ancestress is feeding it. The scratch marks appearing on the belly of the mother during pregnancy or delivery are known as *Ka trud iawbei* (Ancestress scratch). The original hair of an infant not yet one year old is called *U niuh iawbei* (Ancestress hair) and for this reason no knife, scissors or blade should touch the infant's head until it has crossed the age of one full year. If the "Ancestress' hair" is to be cut away it will amount to robbing the infant of *Ka Rngiew*. When cutting or shaving the hair of a child who has crossed the age of one year, a portion of the original which is the Ancestress' or God's hair should be retained.

The birth of twins is believed not to be good. It is thought to signify that the Godhead is offended as also Ka Dawiing. When twins are born in any family, that family must try by divination and consultation, to find out the cause. They believe that these twins are born by splitting of the same life-soul and therefore are to be treated with complete equality down to the minutest detail (e.g. clothing). If this is not done they believe, that the balance on which there lives rest will become upset which might eve result in the death of one of the twins.

Bringing up a child is a delicate and difficult job. Besides preparing and keeping ready the feed for a child, there are many things to attend to. When they go to woods or sit by streams for relaxation or go to the cultivations in the jungles or in the open to work, they do not lay the child on the ground lest any travelling demon on his way should catch the child. They lay down the child in a small hut duly thatched on the sides as well as on the roof and keep an iron knife under the pillow to scare away demons. When taken on the back to any place at night a child must be given a piece of charcoal to hold as the burnt charcoal is the symbol of fire to scare away evil spirits or demons. When a child is taken beyond the outskirts of the village it should touch a young broomstick plant which is not yet flowering. It is strictly prohibited to take a child to a house where they keep *U Thlen* as the "household deity" because this deity will draw away the *ka rngiew* of the child and if the visit with a child is inevitable, a cut piece of a *Mawkhaseng* (a kind of reed from which an arrow was made in ancient times to shoot and kill *U Thlen*) should be fastened to the child thus taken.

Since their childhood children have been taught and trained to behave well, in the house and when they go out. They are taught to be well-behaved and careful in their movements, in their address to relatives or others, in taking their food, in dressing up and so on. They are taught to know and respect their work and duty and also to be aware of the ups and downs in the economic life of the family. They are taught to know and identify their clanmen and the paternal relatives and to show their love and respect to them. They are also taught to love and respect their friends, neighbours and their fellow-villagers. They are taught to realise and note that the respect of the family and the clan is the most important thing for them and wherever they go they must never lose this respect so that the world or people at large will have no cause to speak ill of them or to criticise them.

Children who do not obey their parents are called "disobedient children" and are a worry to the family. Children reflect the family. When they move with dignity in society, the world calls them "dignified children of the family". Parents of such children move in society with joy and pride and their children to them are a wealth. "How many"? we ask anyone, and then, "Are they all right?" is the next question. The Khasi believes that a family with a large number of children is a house which God gives His blessings to and nothing could be happier than this. All the wealth of the world cannot be compared to them; they are the spiritual wealth, and without them a family is not a family at all nor a clan a clan.

## Naming Ceremony

**Plate 13:** The Diviner seeks approval of God for the selected name of the male child

**Plate 14:** The four arrows and the bow that symbolised bravery and courage

**Plate 15:** The diviner directs the baby to be a protector of his clan and womenfolk

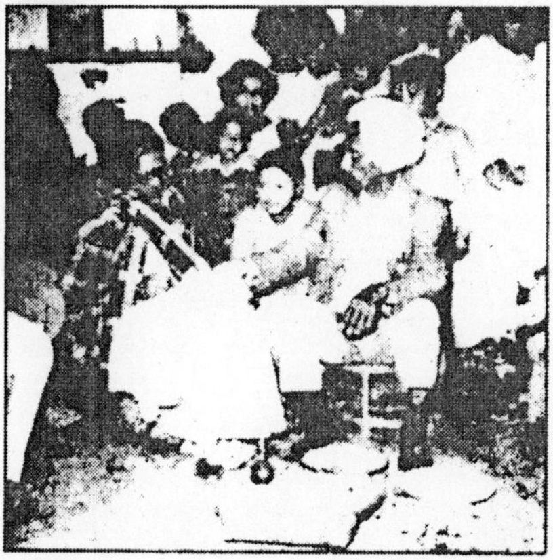

**Plate 16:** Prayers to God in the presence of ceremonial food

**Plate 17:** Reading of signs in the *Khapiah* (fish)

**Plate 18:** The elders mark the left side of the aunt's feet

*Facing page 81*

# 11

## Good Conduct

WHEN a Khasi speaks of *Ka Akor* (demeanour) he usually prefixes it with the complementary or akin word *Ka Buit* (skill) so that the complete phrase is: *Ka Buit ka Akor*. *Ka Buit* stands also for wisdom or knowledge, understanding and the faculty of reasoning and decision-making which enables a man to develop in his profession and his relations with his fellow men. Skill (*Ka Buit*) has a great value but this alone without proper bearing or demeanour (*Ka Akor*) becomes naked and incomplete and its value diminished. Demeanour is that which a man shows outwardly to others as his own nature and therefore the *Akor Khasi* (Khasi demeanour) is that which the Khasi show to the world as their nature.

The Khasi demeanour and the Khasi way of life therefore go hand in hand. We cannot have the Khasi mode of life if we do not have the Khasi demeanour and vice-versa. The Khasi nature is that original nature which exists in him as a Khasi and flows in his blood. Khasi life on the other hand indicates that which he exhibits outside to others as the Khasi nature which he possesses and he does it with the characteristic Khasi demeanour.

The nature of a person expresses itself in his work and other activities, trade and profession, his language, his mode of dressing, his movements and his attitude towards, his fellowmen. All the aspects of a man's life are subject to the laws and traditions given by the ancestors and the Khasi demeanour is embodied in these laws and traditions. If there is *Ka ain Blei* (a law pertaining to God) by which a Khasi should know God and regulate himself in relation to God, there is also *Ka ain briew* (a law pertaining to man) by which a man should know how to regulate himself in his own personal behaviour as well as in relation to his fellowmen.

The idea of *Ka akor* encompasses all aspects of a Khasi's life. A person who does not exhibit *Ka akor* may be Khasi but he has lost the identity of Khasi life since the Khasi demeanour manifests the Khasi life and the latter in turn manifests the Khasi identity. There is a remark that Khasis as a race are extraordinarily conservative in their behaviour. The reason behind this is that the Khasi have inherited from their ancestors a profound desire to preserve their identity in this world. And in spite of tremendous powerful external forces working against this aspiration of the Khasi, they have been able to keep intact their sense of identity as a race.

*Ka akor* enjoins the people to use language, in daily conversation, with dignity. Words used must not be loose, but well-considered, decent and meaningful; they must not bring unpleasantness to or hurt those to whom they are addressed. If we are to use words which might convey unpleasant meanings we must prelude them with an apology by saying something like "As if to convey in an unmannerly way . . . ." We must always select our words carefully—implying our foreknowledge of those to whom we are talking, be they our friends, maternal or paternal relatives. We must also determine and take into account the age of those with whom we are conversing or to whom we are addressing ourselves. The elders or seniors and also those who are our juniors are to be shown the respect due to them. Care should be taken in the manner of expression and choice of words so that what we say is in keeping with one's own sense of dignity and commands the respect of others. We must be particularly careful with our language, when we are talking to strangers or to people with whom we are not on intimate terms.

On the other hand, we must not fight shy of speaking our mind to our fellowmen. We must be frank, as well as sociable and polite in conversation. Inquisitiveness about other people's income, gossipping, meddling in others' affairs and rumour-mongering are not permissible. We must not also speak ill of others in our conversations. Gossipping from door to door and meddling in other people's affairs are like the *Sim-lai-dieng*, mean. When we meet someone known to us, we must shake hands with them and ask after their health and of the members of their family. When we go from place to place, we must talk to all and sundry and not just to our friends. Our expression should be always frank and lucid as an unintelligible expression or circumlocation in daily affairs, implies to a Khasi a freak mind not clear in thought and not clean either in character.

It is not good demeanour to be talkative or to raise one's voice and/or to indulge in bantering. In conversation it is generally advisable not to interrupt others; and when circumstances arise, where one must do so, one must first say .... "Sorry to interrupt you ...." Nobody should walk directly in front of some one who is seated, and if one must do so, one must first apologise by saying "Forgive me for walking past you". We are never to hand or take a thing by the left hand, except when it becomes absolutely necessary to do so; and then we must say .... "Excuse me for using the lefthand". If one accidentally touches somebody with one's foot, one should touch him with the hand and say .... "Please, excuse me". When shaking hands with anyone we must not snatch or pull his hand but only make a slight contact and then raise the fingers a little in an upward direction to convey one's thanks. When one happens to sneeze or yawn in the midst of company, one must apologize by saying ... "How is it so—I'm sorry". Should we need someone and this someone is engaged in conversation with somebody else, we are not to disturb the conversation. We must wait till the conversation has ceased and if, in an emergency, we must intervene, we are to tender a prior apology.

*Ka akor* includes a set of complex instructions in the matter of dress. Any dress not in conformity with the Khasi *Ka akor* is called "an unearthly dress". Instructions in the matter of dress are not so strict in the case of male as compared to a female. The traditional Khasi belief is the female's body is an object of great respect, and therefore, a woman should dress in a manner befitting this respect. She must cover her whole body, and never dress in order to expose or flaunt any part of her body. Her breasts and legs should always remain covered. The hair must be parted at the centre and the hair style should be dignified.

It is not becoming to disturb or obstruct anyone at work.

Should we need others' tools and implements in our work we should ask for permission before using them and take special care of them while we use them and should return them in a courteous way.

In all spheres of his life a Khasi is governed by *Ka akor*. In one sense, it is part and parcel of his existence. If *Ka akor* were to completely disappear it would affect one's very identity as a Khasi and the Khasi people would lose their distinction which will, no doubt bring in social chaos and confusion and ultimately result in the total extinction of the race.

At home *Ka akor* brings love and respect and is the source of harmonious existence. Speaking without due respect to parents might invite a remark from the neighbours like: "What! Why vomit so? Are you not aware that the parents are the Sun and the Moon?" Similarly it binds the relationship between brothers and sisters. Elder brothers and sisters are to be addressed with love and respect and younger ones with love and tender care. The uncles and aunts must also be addressed in a befittingly respectful tone. Outside the home the same demeanour should prevail. Special respect and regard must be paid to the paternal relatives, and special loving regard to the issues of the male clan members. More norms of courtesies and regard are laid down with regard to neighbours, fellow villagers, friends and intimates. Ignorance of these norms reflects the lack of proper guidance and teaching at home.

Some do complain that a Khasi is an extreme stickler for details in matters of etiquette. But this, while it is true, is really a sign of high civilization and culture. A man of good demeanour conquers all. Good demeanour costs nothing but wins all. A man possessed of it never walks alone nor remains alone at any juncture of his life and the world itself shows its gratitude to him.

# 12

# *The Village*

THERE is no distinction of class or caste in traditional Khasi society. As members of society all are equal, have equal rights and obligations, and jointly share the responsibility of running it.

The Khasi shares with other tribes in the world the so called tribalist view of himself in relation to his society. He lives, moves, and as it were, has his being in his tribe. He does not live nor profess all by himself and he who prefers to live by himself is an *outcast* and *U Nongaiksuid.* The true Khasi thinks for himself alone but he lives also for others. He must not isolate himself in spirit and in life from the rest of his tribe : his own kith and kin, his neighbours, his mates and comrades. He seeks other's company and they seek his. He visits them and they visit him. Wherever he goes he exhibits love and respect and receives these in turn. The Khasi are also a race of great good humour and wherever there is a Khasi there is no lack of humour and wit.

On his return from the field the Khasi takes his meal, and then he is out of the house. Only aged men remain indoors. There are homes where they collect together and sit, men and women, around the flaming hearth at the centre of the room. They spend their happy leisure chewing betel nuts, smoking pipes or hookas and rubbing tobacco round their gums. Aged inmates would be snoring away their fatigue in slumber while the rest of the gathering enjoy themselves telling and listening to the legends and stories of their land. Stories having been told, they throw friendly and familiar challenges at one another, or tell jokes which provoke great merriment with men and women laughing to their heart's content and beating and kicking themselves, their faces awash with tears of joy. When the night has gone far and the time to rest has come they separate and depart to their respective huts for retirement. Males leave on their own but females go with neighbours and from one end of the village to another one would hear loud words of farewell and signalling cries to ascertain safe arrivals, renting the air for the while. Then all would be quiet as dead as the night. Early in the morning as soon as the early dawn streaks with the fiery young ball in the sky they get up to set about the new tasks of the new day.

A group of young men may visit a girl's house at night not only because one of them may be in love but because they thereby gain prestige amongst fellow young men; and this also becomes another occasion for jokes and amusement. They sit around the hearth at the centre of the girl's home and for the whole night they exchange friendly jokes in the midst of exuberant laughter. Those who have to yield to slumber, go off to sleep in a corner while the rest continue with their jokes and tell stories till the first cock crows, when they must go home and get ready for the day ahead. The boys do not single out the home of one girl for their nightly visits—but all homes with young maidens must take their turn. Sometimes they visit a house in a neighbouring village. Occasionally music is arranged in some house, and boys and girls sing to the accompaniment of the *duitara* or the *marynthing*. On such occasions the whole village might flock to the house to listen to the music.

When there is anyone sick in a house young men will all go to such a house at night to watch and help take care of the sick throughout the night. In case of death, it is the duty of the whole village to do all the needful in disposing of the dead body. Older people get busy making a bier while strong young men will go to the woods cutting and dressing the big green pines to construct a pyre. The young people carry the dead body to the funeral pyre while the elderly attend to the turning of the body whilst it is burning. This they do after proper ceremony; they also use liquor in the course of their work of turning the dead body. The dead body having been disposed of, they collect the cash amount given to the corpse by friends and relatives, called *Ka bai pynkham* for a round of drinks. At night the youngsters go to the house of the dead person to pass the night with the members of the bereaved family—thereby easing their sense of loss and rendering solace in their bereavement. The next morning they will, in a group, go to wash all the clothes and garments of the bereaved family as well as their own.

When the time for working in the fields comes the youth gather themselves in groups. Thus grouped, they work at all the fields by turn. The family for which they work on any particular day must provide the mid-day as well as the evening meal for all members of the group who eat together with great relish and joy. When someone is not free it does not affect the group—they do not force anyone who cannot join them. This group or community work is practised particularly during sowing and harvesting times. In a body jointly they go to their work—be it in the jungle cultivation or open fields—jointly to sow and jointly to harvest. In case there is a widow or self-supporting female in the village the entire village will set aside one day to help her. Every household must provide at least one adult male for this work. This is done so that nobody in the village has to face starvation or take to begging for a livelihood which will be a matter of shame to the village and to the society at large. If someone is starting a new family and building a new house, the whole village will fix a single day for the work of building the house and generally the hut is completed during the course of the day as the owners would already have made the foundation and have kept all the needful articles ready. What might remain for the owner is to put the necessary finishing touches of polishing and decoration.

People of all age groups, have their respective work at hand and none is free. Their work is their primary duty and there is a different time for merriment; and for that reason seldom can we find an idle person. While hard at work they go on chewing betelnuts, smoking pipes and rubbing tobacco round their gums. In every household they brew rice beer, and it is available in various degrees of maturity. Work does not lie pending, the granary sheds are usually full to the brim and the huts are full of other crops. Hardworking as they are, the Khasis are not lovers of wealth nor do creditors run to them for the repayment of debts. Once every week males will have an archery competition and every now and then during the right season they go for collective hunting. They dress in style when they go to the market place once a week. They go to the market not merely to sell their commodities or to purchase their household necessities but also to meet friends and relatives. Periodically they have their thanksgiving or cultural dances with males and females taking part. Those who have daughters of near marriageable or marriageable age take out their stored garments and silver and gold ornaments and dress their daughters in them so that they can participate in the dances along with others. They take great pride in their own children.

In respect of administration and individual and social justice the Khasi have their own village council (*Durbar*) and this general body elects the village headman and the village elders to help the headman to run the affairs of the village as per the jurisdiction extended to them. Once agreed and decided upon by the Durbar the whole village in a group leave their private work and respond to the call to construct the village or community water places or village paths or such other works pertaining to the enhancement of the village life. On occasions of dispute or quarrel between two or more parties they must not seek a solution by the sword but must listen to the arguments and reasons of their neighbours and fellow-men. When no compromise or satisfactory solution can be reached in this way, they go before the appointed head and elders of the village who will handle the case sympathetically and with understanding. Their effort will be to strike a compromise which will not hurt either party. They must accept the verdict of the elders with humility and good grace.

When some clans perform their ritual of *Thep Mawbah* the whole village is in a mood to celebrate for the ensuing *Ka Phur Ka Siang* and to give themselves up to the joy of community dancing. They would gladly lend a helping hand and heartily take part in any celebration or ceremony in a household of the village or locality.

If there is any trouble-monger in community affairs the villagers will not let him get away. The *Nongaiksuid* are shaved in three positing lines (*khi lai nuid*) and the *Nongshohnoh* are driven away from the village.

All are to obey the regulations and heed the warnings of

the village elders and respect the majority feeling. Those who cannot oblige are not fit to be inhabitants of the village and they should go away. The spirit of unity and common understanding informs the entire community and everybody shares the sense of responsibility in the smooth functioning of the village affairs and for the sake of peace and harmony in the society. The life of the village must be calm and tranquil—its joys and sorrows being shared alike by all.

# 13

# *Administration*

DEMOCRATIC values are deeply embedded in Khasi social life. In the history of the world we find that the landlords are also the people who wield the authority of administration. We see that it has been so in the neighbouring plain areas as well as in distant foreign lands A significant phenomenon throughout the world is that those who wield power exploit the common men through their land tenure system. Such things just do not happen in the land of the Khasi.

The Khasi as a tribe, assume the right of ownership over all the land in their possession. We have nothing to substantiate that the Khasi have conquered this land from others nor to say that other people occupied this land prior to them, as no evidence is available at all. It might be that some other rulers had been ruling this land as part of their kingdom and the Khasi had to shed blood to gain this land and to defend it thereafter. So much blood must have been shed that the land came to be known as *Ka Ri Umsnam* (the Bloodshed Land).

Once the Khasi came to own these hills he never tolerated any one else to trying gain the right of ownership over them. As a safeguard against any such attempts, community life was strengthened by the strict enforcement of "rights and customs". Rights and customs are analogous to religion and rites. Rites may differ and change but religion remains static and cannot change and similarly customs may change but rights remain what they are. Our present generation can change the customs but once the change affects the rights, it has annihilated the very foundation of the Khasi's claim over his land. When he sieves and threshes to establish a custom he does it on the assumption that the whole land under his possession is a community land (*Ri raid*). Any person can acquire any part of the land for his individual use but he should utilise it. This land so used may, after years, become *Ri Kynti* (private land) but if the land is unkept and unutilised it again becomes community land. Neither custom nor tradition allows any one to acquire land without utilising it.

This is the foundation of the Khasi custom with respect to land and the same idea determines that the administration is also based on the right and supremacy of the people. A large clan establishes its own domain or locality where only the clanmen and their close paternal relatives reside. The maternal uncle of the families of clanmen, besides being the custodian of their religious rites is also the man to rule and administer over the social and daily affairs of the village or locality. He becomes the embodiment of the maternal abode of all the clanmen as well as the "father" of his paternal kith and kin. Thus the habitation expands and the territorial occupation is enlarged but the centre of control over the family and social activities remain the same. And the controller or administrator of the original place of foundation is called Basan Shnong (Administrator of the Headquarters-Village) and a Basan Raid (Sub-Administrator) looks after the areas resulting from the splitting of larger units into smaller units of habitation due primarily to the growth of population. These new villages or quarters have their own headmen and eldermen at the village level. All of them manage their own affairs at each respective village level but are under the overall control of the Basan Raid. In some other areas the designation of *Basan Raid* is given to an elected leader known by different names such as *Lyngdoh* mostly in the Bhoi and War areas, *Doloi* among the Pnars (Jaintias).

The Raids constitute their own *Durbar Raid* (*Raid* Assemblies) and the villages have their own *Durbar Shnong* (Village Assemblies). This system forms the basic foundation of Khasi democracy. All administrative matters pertaining to the village are known to the general public. The people choose their own village headmen and elders and these look after judicial and administrative affairs. Matters which cannot be settled by the council of village headman and its elders are put up before the village assembly which finally decides the issue and functions as the ultimate source of authority.

The Syiem's administration is a later phenomenon. Village and Raid affairs gradually multiplied and thus became complicated. The world becomes wider and so also the human experiences of life. The Raid authority by itself gradually finds itself too limited an authority. The Khasi also saw that their neighbouring plains people had an administrative set-up under their 'Rajahs' and some of these were powerful kingdoms. The idea of a similar kingship for themselves gradually evolved in the Khasi mind. They saw the need for establishing kingdoms and of having kings to collect the people together to look after the administration and to dispense justice, to award penalties and even corporal punishment if necessary and to bring to book evil doers, criminals and law breakers in order to maintain peace and harmony. These kings (Syiems) used to be like mothers; they would collect and take care of the destitutes, the abandoned, the orphans, the supportless and also those who have lost their clanmen, whose relatives having all died there is no one left to take care of them. To achieve this aim of formation of a kingdom, therefore, several Raids come together to select a king.

A Khasi knows how to determine the power of the Syiem (king) as well as that of the people in the administration of the state. In all things the power of the people ranks supreme. The Syiem's power is delegated so as not to collide with the supreme authority of the people. A limitation is placed on the power of the Syiem so that he is really no more then a nominal head and ruler of the state. According to the customs and traditions in vogue, therefore, the Syiem in a Khasi state rules but does not hold on to himself the power of the state. Syiems are mere tools of the state and Syiemship is not ultimately an end in itself since the end and supreme power is the people's. In the Khasi political structure the Syiems therefore realise and understand that they are only a part of the state which belongs to the people. Over and above the people there is no other power.

In order to help the Syiem in the administration as well as to safeguard against possible misuse of power entrusted to him, there are also the *Myntris*, *Lyngakors*, *Basans*,

*Lyngdohs* elected from the different clans. These are from those big and dominant clans which constitute and establish the kingdom. Their duty is to help the Syiem in the regular administration of the state. They are called *Ki Bakhraw*. This title does not mean that they have descended from an upper clan as there is no classification of clans or society in our land but it is only a title of distinction given to them as rulers of the state. These, along with the Syiem are also the instruments of the state to run the administration. On top of the Syiem and his *Dorbar* (Council) of *Ki Bakhraw* there is another power or authority which is the supreme authority namely the *Durbar Hima* (State Assembly) and this is the foundation stone of Khasi democracy.

Another name given to this *Dorbar Hima* is *Ka Dorbar Blei* (the Assembly of God). It is so called because the Khasi believes that this Supreme Council or Assembly is extremely powerful and ought to be respected as such and its authority is not to be trifled with. This Dorbar is held only in the *Iingsad Iingsunon* (in any hallowed site). Any person attending the Dorbar understands its sanctity and no one must assume self-importance and show his contempt to others or exhibit temper or tell lies or be drunk. Anyone showing contempt of this Dorbar is taken as a complete misfit who is not even worthy of being physically touched and of such a person they say "Take him away with a winnow, throw into his face burning ashes and swing him out to the farthest ditch".

This Dorbar is also called *Ka Dorbar Laiphew Shong*. This is a very special assembly. It is convened to deal with very important issues like dethroning the ruler (*Syiem*) or selecting a new ruler or the impeachment of the ruler or matters relating to decision about making wars against any other kingdom. This Dorbar is so called because all the representatives and elders of the villages constituting the state are to be present. Each village should be represented by its *Basans* or *Lyngdoh* and also two or three of the village elders who are well conversant with the affairs at hand.

Representatives who are to attend the Dorbar Hima are to be of 50 years of age and above, which ensures that they are mature in thought and in matters of debate, and who are fully conversant with affairs in other places or neighbouring states.

Once the Dorbar is declared to be in session no one is allowed to indulge in private discussion. The chief or ruler (*Syiem*) is the chairman of the session. Once a certain speaker is on the floor none else is allowed to interrupt. The noble assembly or Dorbar listens to reason—accepting the right rejecting the wrong. Prestige, decency and decorum in the proceedings of the debates are strictly maintained. If there is any interruption or apparent discrimination it is only to emphasise the points of reason or order. Once a decision is taken there is no point in registering any note of dissent. Any one who discards what has been decided meets his own fate.

The Dorbar Hima can delegate its authority to the Syiem (chief or ruler) and the *Bakhraw* and they manage the day-to-day administration of law and justice. The authority they embody is commonly known as *the Syiem in Dorbar*. This authority executes the decisions of the Dorbar Hima and the issues over which the Syiem and his Dorbar do not feel competent to take decisions, are placed before the Dorbar Hima. Judiciary is the subject of the Syiem in Dorbar and in judicial matters the rights, customs and traditions of the Khasi people recognised from time immemorial are followed. The Khasi dispensation of justice is "partial" to both sides. The Syiem in his Dorbar hears the arguments of both parties before delivering a judgment. In the course and process of judgment there might sometimes be a dissatisfied reproach by one or both the parties involved in the dispute but by and large they accept the judgment in good grace. The Chief-in-Dorbar reminds the parties involved in the dispute that they belong to the same community of people and that before they submit their dispute to the judicial process they must first try for a compromise settlement. He tries to coax them not to take things too self-righteously as being human none in this world could be perfect. He also reminds them to look at both sides of the coin, but he makes it a point to see that people do not feel insecure from lack of justice at his hand. When there are disputes on matters over which both parties stand adamant and neither is willing to compromise or reconcile, the judicial authority takes resort to *pynkie klong* or *jingiangam um* or "divination for determination of justice".

Besides the Syiem in the Dorbar (or the Council of the Syiem) there are also the *Lyngskors* and the *Basans* looking after their decentralised units and having their respective subordinate judicial authority over those areas. Matters which they cannot settle in their respective areas are then referred to the Syiem in his Dorbar. These units or areas known as *Raids* or *Shnot* have their own respective courts of law. The Lyngskors or Basans are never allowed to function or dispose the cases in their family houses. To turn any wife's residential house into a place to try cases is strictly prohibited by the customs and traditions of the Khasi.

Besides the administration of justice in the court of the state there is also disposal of justice at the village levels. The maintenance of justice and its disposal is also done in a democratic spirit. Each village has a village assembly or council of which every male adult is a member. This assembly of the village elects its village headman or headmen and elders to form a village council to carry out the administrative affairs of the village according to Khasi custom and tradition and as per the directive of the village assembly. The assembly legislates the village decrees and regulations and the headmen and councillors carry them out in their executive authority. Any defaulter violating the regulations specified is brought by the headman and his councillors to the general notice of the assembly as a whole and the village assembly would, then, give due punishment. Any serious intentional violation of the village regulations could lead to the offender's being exiled from the village. Any case of dispute is taken up by the village council consisting of the village headman or headmen and elected leaders and if the council cannot decide, the same is referred to the Syiem in his Dorbar.

The basis of the whole state is the village and the village assembly. It is an assembly of the people who elect their own village headman and elders. This village Dorbar does all that is necessary in matters pertaining to the village administration including the disposal of justice. The Syiem and his Bakhraw are much relieved by this decentralisation of power and in olden times when the world was peaceful, they almost had nothing to do. At that time the duty of the Syiem and his Dorbar was confined only to matters such as administration and control of markets, imposition and collection of levies, duties, royalties and others. A Khasi by nature is not a quarrelsome person or one prone to litigation. For small matters, whatever there may be, they are content to settle things at the level of the village Dorbar.

The Khasi administration and disposal of order and justice is inspired by democratic principles. The people themselves hold the supreme authority. Next comes the Syiem who assumes the role of a mother and whose relation to the people is like a mother's relation to her own children and after him come the Bakhraw who are looked upon as maternal uncles and fathers of the family. The whole state is like a family having a head or a chief for a mother, children, uncles and fathers.

Even today there are countries in many parts of the world which have not attained the democratic form of government and civil strife and bloodshed still flourish. It might, therefore seem strange that the Khasi have known and practised democracy from time immemorial. The Khasi type of democracy has its own peculiarity and cannot be measured by any yardstick which is alien to it.

As a people we believe that the characteristic spirit of Khasi democracy will remain even if there is a change of style and function. The concept of a "representative" which is commonly associated with the idea of democracy nowadays does not have a place in the traditional Khasi framework of democracy. The survival of the traditional spirit of democracy will, therefore, depend upon how successful we are in incorporating this idea into the old framework. For a start, the representatives, elected by the people, must understand and play their roles as the actual uncles and fathers of a family—in spirit and in practice.

# 14

## *Nature—I*

A KHASI lives with nature and nature lives in him. When he thinks all the objects around him such as the animals on the surface of the earth, the winged creatures dominating the earth from above, the flowers on the ground and on the trees, the grass and the vegetation all around—he sees that they have each their peculiar and different lives; and they symbolize for him the tremendously variegated character of man himself. Some things in nature inspire him while some others dishearten him as they remind him of the potentialities of decadence in human nature.

Take for instance, the Khasi's relation with the trees around him and the ubiquitous bamboos. To some trees he is content only to give a name while others frequently acquire a symbolic significance and stories and legends are told about them. The oak tree for instance is anthropomorphised. It is a tall tree with far-flung and strong branches : dominant, progressive, and never prepared to give way. A Khasi cites this tree as the equivalent of a great-hearted man who never surrenders, come what may.

When a Khasi looks at a tender but solid grass spike, this brings to his mind the thought that this sharp spike would one day easily become a bamboo. He marks this capacity for natural objects to grow. But then he also cannot help but think that the growth might not take place at all. The Khasi themselves for instance might eat the shoot. He laments that the poor young shoot just might not know its fate. It grows thinking proudly that it is so strong that it will certainly reach the sky. But nature has shown that there is no such guarantee; and this might be instructive to those foolish.

careless and carefree young men who think that the whole world is theirs for the asking.

A woman who grumbles and complains all the time of her supposed misfortunes is likened to a *Tlai nili kit synrum.* But in a more charitable mood he might liken her to *U dieng byllan, U siej liar-ngot* and similar others.

*Ka diengson babe lado* and *Ka diengphiang Klet hat* are really persons metamorphosed as trees as a result of a romantic tragedy; but the cause of the tragedy was their ignorance and pride.

The stories of the *diengjaminrei-sang-bakha-ieij-kpa-nah* who had to face much shame and trouble and tribulation in her life for her acts of sacrilege and profanity are meant as warnings to the entire people against such acts. Then there are, of course, the marvellous stories about the flower *U Tiewlarun* which is referred to also to as *u tiew larun babun jingriam* (a flower of various attractions).

Orchids provide another fertile ground for comparisons. A *tiew dohmaw* (a rare orchid), embodies all the qualities of a genius, and the name of this flower is also another name for a genius. In a *tiew pathai-khubor* (a very sweet scented flower) a Khasi sees a man of remarkable reputation whose name is a household word. A beautiful *tiew knup-mawsiang* (an orchid known as 'Ladies slipper'—cipripedium) growing in the middle of a cliff or rock evokes the image of a sage who sets himself of as a recluse to escape from the vicissitudes of social life. *Tiew lalyngi pep shad* (another orchid) is a woman of remarkable position and wealth who becomes so involved with the beautification of her own body, her dress, ornaments etc. that she is always a late arrival. The *tiew diengngai* (flower of the iron-tree—Messuaferrea) symbolises a woman who is reckless, and would do anything without fear or shame. The *tiew hur-mari* (beautiful flower hidden under foliage) symbolises a woman who is shy to make a public appearance in spite of her inner strength. *U tiew pathai eitrong* (yellow flower of a pumpkin—cucurbita pepo) which bears no fruit, reminds the Khasi of the life of a person who only aspires for fame and respect without doing anything to deserve these. The flower known as *tiew thanthuni-shong-ri-twa* (a flower to be found in slopes) evokes the image of a fickle-minded woman and the flower known as *tiewjaloi-shong-ri-bajem* (a flower which grows in damp places) symbolises simple minded persons who want always to be in the company of clever, immoral people. The *tiewklong-shong-arnat-diengbah* (a parasitic plant which has roots in more than one tree) is likened to young people who are simple and do not like to meddle in the affairs of others.

Similarly with grasses, herbs and vegetables, a Khasi thinks grimly that there are persons like the *wang bam im* (stalk of a taro-colocasia) who are terribly dangerous. Again, when he comes across a gentle stranger (especially a woman) he cannot but think of the *wang kushu* (stalk of a taro-colocuria): the sort of person who is likely to cause disappointment. And there is great fun in the thought, that in his wide experience of people in society, a Khasi meets persons who are like the *bat iam bait* (a sensitive plant—mimosa pudica), the *jilymphur-eitmut* and the *tiew eit* (flower which does not bear fruit).

Animals are also a source of numerous didactic comparisons. Man's potentiality for lowly behaviour fills the Khasi with shame and he expresses this shame by such phrases as *sew-bna-lat* (a dog reaching every feast), *'sew nguid prie* (a dog eating its own vomit), *miaw bam khun* (a cat devouring its own kittens), *suri ba pynjot* (destructive and callous wolf), *myrsiang sadew* (sly fox) and similar others. Bullocks busy ploughing, are compared to a man who goes on laboriously at his work. Different thoughts cross his mind when a Khasi observes a breeding-bull, a ploughing ox, a goat coaxed to lick salt placed in a leaf. People who flaunt their physical power are thought to be limited as a fowl, cowards are likened to *nai pilang* (large hill rat) and to *kui-pyngkat* (lynx).

Winged creatures similarly evoke images of human qualities compared to the nature of the winged creatures. A Khasi feels great pride to have among his people a man who can be called a *simsong* (a bird whistling very emphatic notes). But he feels despondent to think that in the society there are also people who can be called *ka sim lai dieng* (meddlesome talkative fellow), a *u sim tyngwieng* (water-ouzel) and *proh jyndem* (a crested bird—upupa epops). When he hears and thinks of *u jalyeit* (a small singing bird of green colour) he cannot but think of an eloquent orator. He sees a *moina* (a mynah) when he comes across a person who speaks fluently another language. Then there is the story of the *langwarku sang khyndew* (a green fruit pigeon) who was really a girl, who oppressed by her step-father, swore never to put her feet on the ground again. The sad love story of the *Sohlyngngem shong ri dymmiew* (a large green pigeon) which sings and haunts only the shady parts of the woods and pines for her lover *U Sim Rynniaw* is known to every Khasi. He also tells the story of the *paitpuraw saw tdong* (bulbul) who indulges in much defiance of advice given.

A Khasi learns from a bed-bug that it is foolish to over-bother others for one's own advantage. *Khun tham* (crab's children) or *khun-jynrein* (a louse's child) are wicked people indeed. It is also ungracious and mean to indulge in gossip or uncontrolled talk like a *tyrpud* (big lizard; ant-eater) or to blabber, interfere with others' affairs and get oneself involved physically in anything without knowing or studying the out-come like a *niang thangdoh* (fire fly). It is also foolish to relate with pride something which is impossible or an event that did not actually take place and such a person is therefore called a *sharyntoh* (a mantis). It is also never wise to spend one's time only in merriment, attending all feasts, musical and pleasure meetings, without considering one's own means of livelihood and the leisure that one deserves. Such a person is likened to a *puit tangkuli kynjih mawsiang* (a locust; grasshopper).

It is remarkable in life to find those great and venerable people who are known as *ki 'lur mangkara* (bright stars) and *ki nai-khadsawsynnia* (full moons). But who would even like to hear of those men whom the society calls *ki kyntem niuhmat* (the sloths) whose laziness appears even in their eyes? And who won't shiver at the thought of the *ingkhong shyllang-mat* (man with scorched forehead), a man who betrays his own country? The term *I men suh syntiew* (literally, a female, expert at embroidery) refers, perhaps surprisingly to a pimp. It is indeed a pity for a person to come to a position in life which might provoke the remark "If you stand, you hit the ceiling; if you sit down, the floor is too wet; if you move an inch forward, the heat is too scorching and an inch backward, the cold is too severe". A person has sank to the lowest depths if he deserves to be smeared with *'peisieh* (hot ash) or drenched in *umthet* (washing water) or given grains of rice for the last time (*ai khaw duh*).

# 15

# *Nature–II*

A KHASI lives in nature and learns in its bosom. It teaches and guides him in his daily existence, be it is in his movement from place to place or in his occupation. He has no clock to tell him the hour of the day or a calendar by which he can tell the weeks, months and years, yet his work does not suffer, because it is nature which determines and coordinates the system of his work.

Nature helps him to know when the rains will come. Seeing an ant carrying its food and eggs and clambering up a slope or into any gap in a rock he knows that heavy rainfall will soon follow which will last for six nights and six days or for nine nights and nine days. When he goes fishing in small waters and he sees that fishes spring and flop in the pools then once again he knows that heavy rains are coming. A brilliant circle round the sun also indicates rainfall and the extent of it will correspond to the degree of thickness of the circle. If the sun's circle is thick, during the sowing season, he abandons sowing because the seeds will be damaged by the heavy rush of water to the paddy field. From the water marks on good fallow left on a stone a Khasi cultivator can judge and ascertain if the rains in that year will be light or heavy.

When he goes to forest plantations or to the fields during the afternoon he looks at a flower called *u tiew kheinpor* (time indicating flower), when its petals have closed in, he knows it is time for him to get ready to return home and if he delays he may be endangered by *u nongshohnoh*. When a small insect *niang kynjah* (insect symbolising loneliness) starts making its first noise before sundown he knows he is to collect his tools and start for home lest night falls and danger comes his way.

Even in the village, when the womenfolk see that *u tiew khein-por* and *u tiew shet-ja* (flower indicating time to cook meal) have closed in their petals, they at once know the time has come to start cooking their meals, as the workers in the fields will soon come and meals should be ready for them the moment they reach home.

When the leaves of the Sinul tree and of *ka diengsyrtok* (a kind of soft wood) have fallen, a Khasi knows that summer is due and when a flower called *u tiew khmat syntai* (a flower heralding autumn) has budded and is in bloom he knows that autumn is here. The chirping of various winged insects keeps pace with the rhythm of his work and the seasons. When the *niangkali* (an insect) chirps he knows that it heralds the summer season and similarly when the *niang kongwieng* (a beetle) chirps shrilly he knows that autumn is on. Seeing that the walnut trees or the wild cherry trees are flowering or budding profusely he knows that his cultivation will prosper and bring him the maximum return, and it will be a fruitful year when rice will be abundant and cheap.

In the Nartiang area of Jaintia Hills and also other parts of the district, if a *'leng kpoh* (belly egg—in a ceremony) is laid by a hen in any house the whole village will go for a community hunting, the lucky egg being kept by the family of that house. They start their journey by offering a prayer and the house where the egg was laid should not close its doors till the time of the return of all the members of the hunting party.

A Khasi can have a premonition of imminent dangers and accidents by observing certain sights and changes in nature. For instance, in the War areas on the border, the shrill chirping of of the *kynpait* or of the *kyrkaw* tells a man that there are wicked persons or *nongshohnoh* (murderers) around and by attending to the cry closely, one can even know whether they are close or far from the spot. In the upland areas also people believe in similar natural signs. The *kyrkaw's* (the common crow's) moaning cries give the same warning but it requires a sharpness of mind to understand the signals they convey. Their cryings and crowings warn a person to be ready to defend himself. If a green fruit pigeon hums only once it signals that some house will catch fire somewhere and if it hums twice there will be a death of some old person or of a beloved child. When a dog howls dreadfully at night it means that evil spirits are at large to carry away some human lives.

In those regions where cultivation of paddy is totally dependent on rainfall, the first clap of thunder is a message to the farmer to start ploughing. When an owl hoots softly in the War areas they know that rain is approaching and wild pepper will grow well. The Khasi knows that when the moon is on the wane it is not a proper time to cut bamboo or reeds, for if this is done at this time the bamboo or the reed will not last long. He also knows how to keep track of the season for the movement of *u doh jei* (one of the fishes in the hill streams which comes in groups and is very tasty to eat). He can tell when it will move upstream as well as the time the other fishes will be ready to lay their eggs.

He has also learnt from nature when to plant fruit trees. When he plants betelnuts in the months of May, June and July he plants only 'male-nuts'. Betelnuts with the shape of a spear, pointed at both ends, are called 'male-nuts'. They can withstand the density of water that may collect inside the nursery. Hence they will not perish even if the monsoons are heavy. He plants the seedlings of whatever other male-nut or female-nut he likes after these months as now there is less water. When he plants orange saplings during the months mentioned above he plants the saplings standing straight as the rain is still heavy and the young sapling cannot withstand the heat of the sun; but if he plants them after those months he has to bend the tops of the young plants to the west so that they are directly exposed to the sun since rainfall is less in these months or else they may shrink due to shortage of water and wither.

Nature also tells a Khasi of any impending sad news. When a snake crosses his path ahead, in course of his travel to any place for a particular purpose, he knows his purpose will not be fulfilled. If he is going to get medicine he will not get it nor will he meet the person he set out to meet. It is particularly bad if the snake happens to be a cobra because the news it portends might even be that of death. However good things may happen if a snake crosses from the right to the left and also if it goes on its own way.

Falling trees or branches of trees are generally bad omens. If it so happens that a tree or branch of a tree just collapses while one is looking at it, one must at once go and examine whether there is any natural decay or any mark of its getting loose. If there is no such thing, he believes this is a sign given to him. If the falling takes place from the right side something sad will happen to his paternal relatives and if it is from the left side something will happen to his clan-members. When he sees a stone rolling down from its position, he goes to look at it. If the falling takes place because of the looseness of the earth or of its support, then it is only natural and this is a commonplace event; but if the base is still firm and there is no indication that it should have fallen, he believes it to be a bad omen. If the falling is from the right side or from the left side, the effect will be as indicated above—respectively to the paternal relatives and the clan-members. If any household has a cock which crows at odd times the belief is that misfortune will befall the household and to prevent that they generally kill the cock by twisting its neck. There is a well regulated time for all things. When a cock crows at an inappropriate time he violates this principle of regularity but its violation is an indication of "irregularity" in its owners.

Nature for a Khasi is like a book. The teaching and wisdom he derives from it, he makes use of in his daily life. He examines meticulously, and with great care the objects around him. He cares for and treasures all he sees and observes so that they could be of help to him in all his needs. Nature is also like a big hospital on whose threshold all types of medicines are to be found which can heal all bodily ailments. Medicine and reason complement one another and a Khasi is not thus helpless. He lives peacefully in his own land and enjoys the embrace of nature.

# 16

# *Folk Tales—I*

THE mode of Khasi thought can also be seen in their folk tales. The stories centre round things and objects seen conspicuously in nature relating them to events and experiences of human life. The stories are told not only for amusement but also for the purpose of giving moral lessons, advice and instruction to the story teller's kith and kin as well as to future generations. To impart instruction directly or similarly to give advice is easy but it is difficult for those to whom the instruction or advice is given to understand or follow them, nor is it easy for them to retain the same in their mind. The Khasi knows that tales and stories are easily remembered and that they should be interesting and should be told with skill and love. The fact that the tales have survived for so long speaks of the care and intelligence which have gone into their making.

There are many methods of teaching each having its own value and effect but perhaps the most simple and effective method of teaching a child or even an adult is through stories. Think of Jesus Christ and His method of teaching through parables. This method has been used also by other great world teachers. It is so because the stories are sweet to hear, easy to understand and to remember and at the same time amusing and interesting.

The Khasi folktales and stories are of various kinds and embody different layers of thought and for that reason the lessons they convey relate to different aspects of human life and enlighten his variegated experience of life.

One of the stories embodying various levels of thought is the story of *U Sier Lapalang* (a stag from the lowland area of Lapalang near Dawki). This stag of many parted antlers, with all his strength and ambition, wants to roam and see the world. He lives in the valleys of the plains with his mother who loves him so much. When he looks upward from the plains to the hills the untold beauty and splendour of these hills move him and a thought and an ambition worked fast in his mind to venture on to these hills. He looked at his antlers and saw them dancing and floating in the air, he felt his breast and it heaved and sighed and looking to his legs he saw them bouncing in the air. He felt that nothing could obstruct or hinder him. He whispered his ambition to his mother but she did not permit him, saying, "Oh my son, do not go to Khasi land, the land where human beings live, stay and stick here in our plains and valleys; and let us have the noımal reed for our food".

Such conflicts take place in every household. A grown up and determined son is apt to aspire for adventure and when a mother forbids him he wants to know the reason. A mother cannot always give a convincing reason and just says, "only because my heart does not feel at ease, my son". *U Sier Lapalang* who was terribly excited in his mind saw no reason why his mother should stop him. He argued with himself but could not satisfy himself. The mother looked at her son and was deeply grieved. She would not say anything—she just grieved and tears came flowing down her cheeks. And who can dare say a word ? When the ambition of the son and the tears of the mother are at war with each other, who will dare to rise up in judgment ?

A Khasi believes that when his mother is not happy with him, he can never prosper. *U Sier Lapalang* set out from his hearth and home without the blessings of his mother on his adventure, and on reaching the hills he fell down on his face. He suffered a violent death far away from home and from his mother who loved him beyond all measure. One might ask, "Could his death be due to the fact that *U Sier Lapalang* disobeyed his mother?" The story does not give any final judgment but leaves it to us to think over.

But what moves a Khasi most in this story is the character of the mother of *U Sier Lapalang*. If there is a mother amongst all the mothers in this world it is the mother of *U Sier Lapalang*. She knows the distance of the hills and the tediousness of the journey and the dangers lurking in it. Yet for the sake of her own son she is not mindful of these. The son has become disobedient but she forgets it all and makes the journey to the hills. When she reaches the hills she knows that her only son is no longer in this world. She heard the shrill cries of the men and knew that very soon they will shoot arrow through her son's heart. She breaks into a painful lament for her son who was the dearest thing she had.

The crowd of bowmen on seeing her became ready once more hoping to bag another deer. A hunter took his aim to shoot the prey in the heart but suddenly came to a benumbed halt when he heard her agonising and heart-rending laments. He listened to the words narrating her terrible story and his stout heart melted with remorse. He lay down his bow and removed the arrow to keep it back in its quiver, as it is an unforgivable offence to harm a widow, or a forlorn and unprotected woman. He bowed down his head and retraced his steps. It is said that, only after hearing the lament of *Ka Sier Lapalang* (the mother) that the Khasi learned to wail and mourn at times of death and only those who have personal experience of death can fully understand this.

Then there is the tale of *Langwarku* or *Langbyrkaw* (green fruit pigeon). The fact that the bird never alights on the ground is good enough material for the plot of the story called *Ka langwarku sang khyndew*. The story goes that there were two sisters who became fatherless. The mother looked after them. They lived happily with her and in their childhood they did not understand much of the loss of their father. The mother on the other hand took the loss to heart; and alone she cannot earn enough to feed and provide for the children adequately. She is also still young and feels lonely at times. A time comes when she considers it proper and gets married a second time.

However, when the step-father comes to live in the house it spells doom for the sisters. He beats them up to his heart's content and denies them food till they start looking like skeletons. Gradually the poor kids become extremely weak in body and they resolve not to tolerate the step-father's ill-treatment any longer. One day when the step-father was away with their mother in the fields, the sisters pulled out whatever feathers they could get from the fowls and stuck them on their bodies. They did so only to fly away. And they became two green fruit pigeons. At once they took to their wings and flew to a nearby tree. From then on the sisters stayed on the branch and decided never again to set foot on the ground. They waited for their mother's return to tell her that the woods henceforth would be their home. The mother pleaded with them to return to her but her bitter cries and showers of tears were in vain. They flew away never to come back again.

The existence of characters like this step-father is a shame in the tribe. "Warku ! Warku !" the call of the fruit pigeon will always remind the Khasi of such sordid characters as long as the sun shines by day and the moon by night.

# 17

## *Folk Tales—II*

KING Solomon of the Bible, the *Book of Proverbs*, says that pride precedes a fall. A Khasi knows this truth, and he wants to instil it in the minds of his children, his sisters, nephews and nieces. The story of the river Umngot and the river Umiew is about pride. They challenged each other once to a race to the *Ri Dkhar* (Surmah Valley). Both sister rivers flow from Shillong Peak. River Umngot, being the younger sister, says in all modesty that she will flow through easy and soft terrains even though she will have to cover a longer distance. But the river Umiew says, "On the other hand, I will negotiate the cliffs and hard terrains, dash against the hills and rocks and see who could withstand me. . ." When River Umngot has reached the *Ri Dkhar*, she turns to look at the hills to see whether river Umiew has arrived. When she is satisfied that her sister has not yet arrived she proceeds on her way but at a slower pace so that her sister could catch up with her. The river Umiew does not appear for a long time and meanwhile the Umngot circles her leisurely way round the river Rupatylli but only till the sister arrives. The failure of river Uniew to arrive first is due to her pride and boastfulness. On seeing that the Umngot river had reached she was overcome with great self-remorse. Her unhappiness is greater because she had boasted in arrogant words and because the Umngot happens to be her younger sister. The tale has it that she cried wretchedly and her convulsions were so great that she broke into pieces, and eventually became five rivers, namely, the Dwara, the Umtang, the Kumarjani, the Prasbiria and the Umtarasa. Through them she loses herself in the Surmah, never to be seen again.

In the Pnar areas (Jaintia Hills) there is a story of a similar challenge between Umngot and River Myntdu as to who will first reach *Ri Dkhar* (Surmah Valley). In the Ri Bhoi Region (Khasi Hills area bordering Assam Valley), a similar story of arrogance and challenge between the Umiam Khwan and the river Umngot is told. The moral of all such tales is that arrogance can never pay and that boastfulness leads to nothing but destruction.

Another familiar story is that of U Manik Raitong. The king of Raitong left his village to collect taxes and royalties from the neighbouring *Ri Dkhar* (Kamrup area in the Brahmaputra Valley) and left behind his wife Mahadei. He had to stay away for a long time, and by the time he returned home his wife had already delivered a son. When it was found out that it was U Manik Raitong who was the father of the child, the Dorbar (king's council) decided to punish U Manik Raitong by burning him alive. U Manik Raitong accepted that verdict with satisfaction For the purpose they constructed a funeral pyre on Raitong Hill. On the appointed day U Manik dressed himself in his best attire, closed his house and proceeded to the pyre, flute in hand, playing sad, touching music.

Mahadei spied everything from her house. Her heart sank, her eyes were filled with tears as she realised that she must share Manik's woeful fate. When Manik reached the funeral pyre he encircled it three times, planted his flute upside down on the ground and threw himself into the flames. A crowd of countless people watched the scene. When the flame was at its highest Mahadei who had come stealthily emerged suddenly from the crowd and jumped into the pyre to die along with Manik Raitong. And it is said that out of the bamboo flute (*Ka Sharati*) which Manik planted on the ground upside down before he jumped into the fire, a bamboo shoot came and till today the branches of this bamboo are upside down.

Manik's bamboo flute is of the kind which is smoked and dried above the fireplace before it is ready to use. The ideal *dao* and knife are used to make it and the holes are drilled with a red hot iron poker.

The king leaves home to attend to his duties leaving his Mahadei behind to look after the house. On his return, after a long absence he finds that some immoral acts have been committed to defame the royalty. Manik Raitong's flute thus symbolised, the lopsided characters of people like U Manik Raitong and Mahadei whose lives were vitiated by profound moral reversion.

It is said that once even in the valley lying between Umniuh Tmar and Nongjri such a bamboo with reversed branches did grow and people of the area tell of similar tales.

Another story is that about U Kyllang and U Symper, two hills in the Khadsawphra Nongkhlaw Syiemship. These hills are not very far apart and they are said to be brothers. Men all round the area also look to them with respect as their *ki ryngkew ki basa* deities worshipped by a group of people who offer them animal sacrifices. But it is said that once there was a struggle for predominance between them and each wanted to be superior to the other so as to get more from their human worshippers. A quarrel ensued and the brothers took to physical combat. They hurled mud and stones at each other till both were injured and the marks of these injuries remain till today. The moral of the story is that brothers must never quarrel or wage war against one other. The disfiguring of both these hills, is a reminder of the permanent misfortune that may befall a family where such quarrels take place.

It is the habit of the peacock to spread and flap his wings at every sunrise and this occasions another tale. It is said that in olden times the peacock was the sun's husband and lived happily with her. But one day while gazing down from the sky at the world below he chanced to see a beautiful garden of flowering mustard plants dancing in the breeze. He took it to be a beautiful maiden and wanted to come down himself to have a close look at this beauty. For a while he kept his desire to himself but the more he looked at her the more he was bewitched. At last he told his wife, the sun. She in turn begged him lovingly not to part from her and not to be carried away. But as he would not listen to her pleas she allowed him to go. He left his rich palace where he lived in great luxury with the sun and reached this world only to find that he was befooled. What he thought to be a beautiful maiden turned out to be a mustard field. He repented and longed to return to the sun, but he could not do so. The round *eye* in the feathers of his tail are the tears of the sun, and the flapping of the wings as soon as he notices the sun's rays in the morning is his memory of the old happiness and his longing to return to her.

The moral of the tale or at least one of the morals is that all that glitters is not gold and that only chaos can result from being swayed by ostentation and wanton display. The peacock found out the truth but it was too late and was doomed to a life of frustration and longing.

In the *Ri Bhoi* area (North-East Khasi Hills District) bordering Assam there is a story where water and fire appear as sisters; water the elder and fire the younger. It is the general belief that it is the younger sister who is the more resourceful in any deal; and so one day fire told her sister, "Dear sister, let us go around and see the outside world, being confined indoors is tiresome. . . ." Water agreed and said, "Yes, it is right, dear sister; where do you want to go?" Fire answered, "On my part, I would go all around. Down the glades and up the hills. I'll go and I am not afraid of any one. I am not afraid of the sun, I am not afraid of the moon. But only two things I am afraid of you my elder sister and human beings". Water in her turn said, "On my part, if I go down the plains I will avoid the rocks, I will avoid the hills and do my best to find the soft and easy way". So they both started from home for a world of adventures and both kept their word.

# *Index*